THE
DANGEROUS
SUMMER

ERNEST HEMINGWAY

Introduction By
JAMES A. MICHENER

SCRIBNER
New York London Toronto Sydney

Thanks to Joan O'Connor, the John F. Kennedy Library,
A. E. Hotchner, Russell Burrows, and to the Tinker Library of the
Spanish Institute of America for research assistance.

SCRIBNER
1230 Avenue of the Americas
New York, NY 10020

First Scribner trade paperback edition 2004

SCRIBNER and design are trademarks of Macmillan Library
Reference USA, Inc., used under license by Simon & Schuster,
the publisher of this work.

Manufactured in the United States of America

17 19 20 18 16

The Library of Congress has cataloged this edition as follows:

Hemingway, Ernest, 1899–1961.
The dangerous summer / Ernest Hemingway : introduction by James
A. Michener.—1st Touchstone ed.
p. cm.
Originally published: New York: Scribner, 1960.
"A Touchstone book."
Includes index.
1. Hemingway, Ernest, 1899–1961—Journeys—Spain. 2. Spain—
Description and travel. 3. Bullfights—Spain. 4. Ordonez Araujo,
Antonio, 1932– 5. Dominguin, Luis Miguel, 1926– 6.
Bullfighters—Spain—Biography. 7. Authors, American—20th
century—Biography. I. Title.
PS3515.E37Z464   1997
818'.5203—dc21 [B]
97-18113 CIP

ISBN 978-0-684-83789-5

CONTENTS

CONTENTS

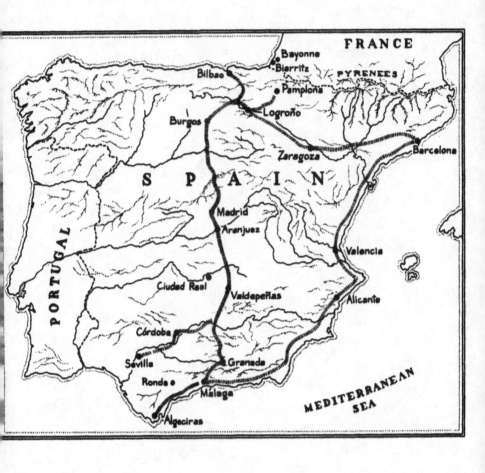

THE
DANGEROUS
SUMMER

INTRODUCTION

JAMES A. MICHENER

THIS IS A BOOK ABOUT DEATH WRITTEN BY A LUSTY SIXTY-year-old man who had reason to fear that his own death was imminent. It is also a loving account of his return to those heroic days when he was young and learning about life in the bull rings of Spain.

In the summer of 1952 *Life* magazine headquarters in Tokyo dispatched a courier to the front lines in Korea with an intoxicating message. After prowling the mountainous terrain along which desultory action was taking place, he found me at a forward post with a small detachment of Marines.

"*Life* is engaged in a tremendous venture," he told me in conspiratorial whispers. "We're going to devote an entire issue to one manuscript. And what makes the attempt so daring, it's fiction."

"By who?"

"Ernest Hemingway."

The name exploded in the cavelike foxhole with such

force, such imagery, that I was instantly hooked. I had always admired Hemingway, considered him our best writer and certainly the man who had set free the English sentence and the crisp vocabulary. As I wandered about the world I constantly met foreign writers who went out of their way to assure me that whereas they considered themselves as good as Hemingway, they did not want to mimic him. They had their own style and were satisfied with it. And I began to wonder why they never said: "I don't want to write like Faulkner . . ."— or Fitzgerald, or Wolfe, or Sartre, or Camus. It was always Hemingway they didn't want to copy, which made me suspect that that's precisely what the lot of them were doing.

If you had asked me the day before that meeting with the *Life* man I'd have said: "I admire Hemingway immensely. He gave us all a new challenge. But of course I don't want to write like him."

The emissary continued: "With so much riding on this experiment *Life* can't afford to take chances."

"On Hemingway? How could you lose?"

"Apparently you haven't been following the scoreboard. The critics murdered his last offering."

"*Across the River and Into the Trees?* It wasn't too hot. But you don't condemn an artist for one . . ."

"That's not the point. They not only blasted the novel, which was pathetic, but they called into question his legitimacy, his right to publish any further."

"I can't believe that."

"Didn't you read that savage burlesque of him and his novel? That hurt."

"I missed it, being over here. But you can't burlesque a man unless he's very good to begin with . . . unless readers are so familiar with his work that they catch the jokes. You don't waste your time teasing a nothing."

"This wasn't teasing. This was a thrust at the jugular."

"Hemingway probably told them to go to hell."

"Maybe, but he was deeply hurt. And *Life* is painfully aware that the attacks cast a shadow over whatever he publishes next." The man paused to study the battlefield in front of our dugout, then came to the point: "We have one hell of a bundle—money, prestige—riding on this one-shot issue."

"Why come to see me?"

"We want to present the story in the best possible light."

"What can I do? I don't know Hemingway."

"Do you respect him?"

"He's one of my idols."

"That's what the editors hoped." He looked me in the eye, then said: "They want you to read the galleys . . . make up your own mind . . . no pressure from us. And if you like what you see, give us a statement we can use in nationwide publicity."

"To what purpose?"

"To kill any lingering reminders of those savage reviews. Knock in the head suspicions that the old man might be through."

"Tell me the truth. Have you asked other writers better known than me? Have they refused?"

"I really don't know. But I do know the editors think that your approach to war and the role of men makes you eligible. Also, they think readers will listen."

"Is Hemingway in on this?"

"He would be mortified if he knew we thought he needed help. He'll know about it when he sees the copy."

The decision was easy and automatic. I assured the emissary that I would read the manuscript, praying that it would be good, and if it was I would not hesitate to say so boldly. Because a writer just getting into his career as

I then was rarely has an opportunity to pay tribute to one of the masters.

"Guard this with your life," the emissary said. "This is the only copy outside New York. And if you decide to make a statement, get it to us in a hurry." Placing the rather frail parcel in my hands, he nodded, warned me not to leave it where others might spy, and left to catch the Tokyo plane.

The next hours were magic. In a poorly lighted corner of a Marine hut in a remote corner of the South Korea mountains I tore open the package and began reading that inspired account of an old fisherman battling with his great fish and striving to fight off the sharks which were determined to steal it from him. From Hemingway's opening words through the quiet climaxes to the organlike coda I was enthralled, but I was so bedazzled by the pyrotechnics that I did not trust myself to write my report immediately after finishing.

I knew that Hemingway was a necromancer who adopted every superior Balzacian trick in the book, each technical device that Flaubert and Tolstoy and Dickens had found useful, so that quite often his work seemed better than it really was. I loved his writing, but he had proved in *Across the River and Into the Trees* that he could be banal, and I did not want to go out on a limb if he had done so again.

But as I sat alone in that corner, the galleys pushed far from me as if I wished to be shed of their sorcery, it became overwhelmingly clear that I had been in the presence of a masterpiece. No other word would do. *The Old Man and the Sea* was one of those incandescent miracles that gifted writers can sometimes produce. (I would learn that Hemingway had dashed it off in complete form in eight weeks without any rewriting.) And as I reflected on its perfection of form and style I found myself comparing it with those other gemlike novellas that had meant so much to me: Edith Wharton's *Ethan Frome*, Joseph Conrad's *Youth*, Henry James's *The Aspern Papers*, and Faulkner's *The Bear*.

When I had properly positioned Hemingway's tale among its peers I hid the galleys beneath my bedroll and walked out into the Korean night, agitated by this close contact with great writing, and as I picked my way across the difficult terrain I made up my mind that regardless of what critics sager than I had said about Hemingway's previous fumbles, I would have to flaunt my opinion that *The Old Man* was a masterpiece, and to hell with caution.

I am embarrassed to state that I have no record of what I actually reported. My judgment appeared in full-page ads across the country, and I think I said something about how happy writers like me were that the champ had regained the title. No one reading my words could doubt that here was a book worth immediate reading.

At any rate, *Life* used my statement enthusiastically and paid me, but what I didn't know was that while their Tokyo agent was handing me my top-secret copy of the galleys—"the only set outside New York"—*Life* was distributing another six hundred sets to opinionmakers across the United States and Europe, each one top secret and unique. When the issue containing Hemingway's novella appeared during the first week of September 1952, it was already an international sensation. One of the cleverest promotions ever orchestrated had resulted in immediate sales of 5,318,650 copies of the magazine, the swift rise of the book version to head the best-seller list, and a Nobel Prize.

Hemingway had won back the championship with a stupendous ninth-round knockout.

The success of this daring publishing venture had a surprising aftermath. *Life* was so pleased with its coup that the editors decided to try their luck a second time, and when they cast about for some writer who might do another compact one-shot, they remembered the man who had stuck his neck out when they needed a launching statement for their Hemingway.

Another emissary, this time from New York with lots of corporate braid, came to see me, in Tokyo I believe, with a dazzling proposal: "We had such an unprecedented success with *The Old Man* that we'd like to go back to the well again. And we think you're the man to do it."

"There aren't many Hemingways around."

"On your own level you might do it. You understand men in action. You have any stories in the back of your mind?"

I have always tried to answer such questions forthrightly. I love writing. I love the swirl and swing of words as they tangle with human emotions. Of course I had a dozen ideas, most of them worthless when inspected closely, but a couple of them seemed to have real staying power.

"I've been doing some combat flying over Korea . . ."

"At your age?"

"And a lot of patrol work on the ground. I see certain big outlines."

"Like what?"

"Like it's perilous for a democracy to engage in war without declaring war. Like it's morally wrong to send young men into action while old men stay home and earn a bundle without any war taxes or deprivations. And it is especially wrong to call a few men arbitrarily into action while allowing others just as eligible to stay home free."

"Would your story be beating those drums?"

"I don't beat drums."

"Write it. I think we might have something."

Driven by a fire I had rarely known, and excited by the prospect of following in the shoes of Ernest Hemingway, I put aside all other work. On 6 July 1953 *Life* offered its second complete-in-one-issue novella, *The Bridges at Toko-ri*. This was less than a year after the great success of *The Old Man* and, as before, the editors protected themselves by asking another writer to authenticate the legitimacy of their offering. This time they chose Herman Wouk to say good things, and although I cannot remember what I said about Hemingway, I recall quite clearly what Wouk said about me: "His eyes have seen the glory." That became the sales pitch this time, but a friend of mine writing a review for the *New York Herald Tribune* phrased it more cautiously:

> This is, says an advance publicity release, "the first major work of fiction to be written expressly for *Life*." We are not sure whether they mean they *ordered* a major work of fiction from Mr. Michener, who duly complied, or that the novel happily turned out to be a major work of fiction after it was completed. We are not even sure, for that matter, whether it *is* a major work of fiction . . .

Although the sales of my effort did not come close to matching those of Hemingway's, the second try was sufficiently rewarding to start the editors looking for a third and a fourth successor, thinking that this could become a yearly ritual. I believe they planned to keep the daisy chain going: me to applaud Hemingway's effort, and then write my own; Wouk to applaud mine and then to write his, and whoever cheered Wouk to write the fourth. Alas, Wouk had nothing in the works that he wished to throw into the race, so *Life* hit upon a British writer with a reputation almost equal to Hemingway's, but his novella fell on its face disastrously, and Number

Four was abandoned. *Life*'s one-shot innovation worked sensationally with a vintage Hemingway. It was moderately acceptable with someone like me, and a flop if the writing was not both inspired and compact. The experiment died.

I met Hemingway only once. Late one wintry afternoon in New York my longtime friend Leonard Lyons, columnist for the *New York Post* and a sometime confidant and travelling companion of Hemingway's, called me: "Papa's up from Cuba. We're here with Toots. Come on over."

When I reached the famous bistro I found Shor in his favorite corner dispensing insults: "Imagine a man of my substance wastin' a whole day with this bunch of writin' creeps." Hemingway, Lyons, and two gofers whose names I did not catch were trading war stories, and although Leonard had assured me that Papa wanted to see the man who had stuck his neck out in defense of *The Old Man*, Hemingway made no mention of that fact; indeed, he was so self-conscious and rude that he even refused to acknowledge that I had joined the party.

Two exchanges softened him. At one point he said, referring to my hometown: "I never wanted to be known as 'that gifted Philadelphia writer.' I wanted to go up against the champions, Flaubert, Pío Baroja." He was astonished when I said that I had once paid my respects to Baroja, a down-to-earth novelist whom I held in great regard. Shortly before Baroja's death, Hemingway had told the salty old man: "You deserved the Nobel Prize, not me." And we spoke affectionately of this hard-grained Spaniard.

More surprising to Hemingway was the fact that I had once travelled with a cuadrilla of Mexican bullfighters, and he was delighted to learn that I had known the

Mexican greats: Juan Silveti with his cigar, fearless Luis Freg, drowned in a boat accident in Mérida, Carnicerito de Méjico, killed in the bull ring, the superb Armillita with no chin and never a major goring, the gaudy Lorenzo Garza, the engaging Silverio Pérez.

We spent some time with these matadors, Hemingway condemning most of the Mexicans to second category, but then I happened to mention the Spaniard Cagancho, the flamboyant gypsy whom Hemingway had respected for the man's unashamed cowardice. This led to a discussion of the corridas I had seen in Spain as a university student on vacation, and when he learned that at my first fight in Valencia—Domingo Ortega, Marcial Lalanda, El Estudiante—I had fallen under the spell of Ortega, a dour, hard fighting man, he told Toots: "Any man who chooses Domingo as his hero knows something," and I told him: "When I was last in Madrid for San Ysidro, Ortega was advisor to the presidente and remembering me from when I trailed along behind him he invited me to join him in the palco."

Hemingway nodded approvingly, but he could not bring himself to thank me for what I had said about *The Old Man*, nor did I wish to bring up the subject. Not long after, in July 1961, I heard that he was dead at the age of sixty-one.

The last extended work of any importance that Hemingway wrote was another assignment for *Life*, and one can visualize the clever editors of that magazine at some strategy session in 1959 proposing: "Wouldn't it be great if we could get Hemingway to bring his bullfighting book up to date?" All present, remembering the great success *Life* had had with *The Old Man*, must have jumped at this suggestion, and when it was presented to Hemingway he must have liked it, too.

In 1930 he had published in *Fortune* a longish, knowing article on bullfighting as a sport and an industry and this led, two years later, to the remarkable illustrated essay *Death in the Afternoon*. A disaster with the critics, who could not understand why a writer of his talent should waste himself on such arcane material, it quickly became a cult book.

Those of us who liked bullfighting recognized this as a loving, faithful, opinionated account of an art form which few non-Spanish speakers understood. We applauded his daring in bringing it to an indifferent public, and we knew it was destined for a long subterranean life. It was one hell of a book.

Succeeding decades had seen it climb to respectability, with Scribners selling hundreds of thousands of copies and reprinting it dozens of times. As bullfighting became popular, with several motion pictures of merit gaining it new adherents, *Death in the Afternoon* became a kind of Bible, with library aficionados who had never seen a fight ardently debating the relative accomplishments of Belmonte, Joselito, and Niño de la Palma. I had kept the book with me in Mexico when I travelled with bullfighters.

In 1959 Hemingway went back to Spain and during that long, lovely summer when he was already beginning to suffer the ravages which would in the end destroy him—monomania about being spied upon, suspicion of his most trusted friends, doubt about his capacity to survive—this powerful man, so much a legend of his own creation, returned to the vibrant scenes of his young manhood. With great good luck he arrived in Spain just as two wonderfully handsome and charismatic young matadors, brothers-in-law, were about to engage in a protracted mano a mano, hand-to-hand duel, which would carry them and their partisans to most of the famous bull rings in Spain.

The matadors were Luis Miguel Dominguín, thirty-three years old and usually the more artistic, and Antonio Ordóñez, twenty-seven, the brilliant son of Cayetano Ordóñez (who fought under the name Niño de la Palma), whom Hemingway had praised in *Death in the Afternoon*. Fairly matched in skill and bravery, they were sure to put on a stupendous show. It proved to be a glorious summer, a most dangerous one, and Hemingway adopted that concept for the title of his three-part series, *The Dangerous Summer*.

Certain facts about the manuscript he produced are significant. *Life* had commissioned him to write a crisp, 10,000-word article about what it was like to go back, but he became so obsessed by the drama of the summer—much of which he superimposed upon a solid base—that he was powerless to halt the flood of words. The first draft ran to 120,000 words. The polished manuscript, from which the *Life* excerpts and the present book were edited, ran to about 70,000. The present version, which contains about 45,000 words, endeavors to give the reader an honest rendering of what was best in this massive affair.

I cannot be critical of the vast amount of overwriting Hemingway did—120,000 words when 10,000 were all that was needed—because I often work that way myself. I have consistently turned in to magazines and newspapers three to four times the number of words requested, prefaced by the note that will accompany these pages when I submit them to Scribners:

> You are invited to edit this overlong manuscript to fit the space available. You are well-regarded editors and cutting is your job.

Even in the writing of a novel I persistently write more than is required, then cut back toward the bone. When a recent publication asked me for six sharp pages on a pressing topic, I warned them: "In six pages I can't even say hello. But I'll invite you to cut."

I wish I could have heard what went on in *Life*'s editorial offices when they saw what their request for 10,000 words had produced. A friend once sent me a photostat of a marginal note which had appeared on one of my submissions to a different magazine: "Somebody ought to tell this son-of-a-bitch that he's writing for a magazine, not an encyclopedia."

What *Life* did was to employ Hemingway's good friend and travelling companion A. E. Hotchner to edit the manuscript, cutting it ferociously. Intended originally as a one-shot nostalgic essay, it would appear as a three-part extended account of the peripatetic duel between the two matadors. I have been permitted to see Hemingway's original version of Part II of the *Life* series and can say with certainty that no magazine could have published the entire version. No book publisher would have wanted to do so either, because it was redundant, wandering in parts, and burdened with bullfight minutiae. I doubt if there will ever be a reason to publish the whole, and I am sure that even a reader who idolizes the author loses little in the present version of the book. Specifically, I think Hotchner and the editors of *Life* did a good job in compressing Hemingway's outpouring into manageable form, and I believe that the editors of Scribners have done an even better job in presenting the essence in this book.

I was in Spain following the bulls shortly after the *Life* series appeared under the agreed-upon title *The Dangerous Summer*, so I was in a position to evaluate its acceptance by the international bullfighting public, a suspicious, envious lot. Men and women alike took strong stands, and the consensus seemed to be: *It was great that Don Ernesto came back. He reported the temporada enthusiastically. He was too partial to his favorite boy. And he should be stood against the wall and fusilladed for the things he said about Manolete.*

It is generally agreed among bullfight fans that the two greatest matadors of recent history have been Juan Belmonte, the twisted little gnome of the 1920s, and Manolete, the tall, tragic scarecrow of the 1940s. Some add the Mexican Carlos Arruza, dead before his time, and bobbysoxers and tourists from France deem the recent phenomenon El Cordobés worthy of inclusion, although purists dismiss him with contempt because of his excessive posturing.

For an American outsider like Hemingway, no matter his long service to the art, to barge into Spain and denigrate Manolete was like a Spaniard sticking his nose into Augusta and claiming that Bobby Jones did not know how to play golf. I heard some extremely harsh indictments, including threats in the tapa bars to beat up on Hemingway if he dared to show his face, but as time passed the castigation became less severe until even Manolete's partisans acknowledged that to have had a Nobel premiado like Hemingway treat their obsession seriously, and in a magazine of *Life*'s circulation, was a desirable thing. Don Ernesto was re-enshrined as the patron saint of the art.

More serious, I think, was the charge that in reporting upon the mano a mano between the brothers-in-law Hemingway had abused the position of the writer by siding so outrageously with one of them, Ordóñez, whom he knew best and obviously idolized. Again and again he betrayed his partisanship—which was justified by the awesome performances of his man—in sentences that an impartial reporter should not have used: "I do not know what Luis Miguel (Dominguín) did nor how he slept the night before the first decisive fight at Valencia. People told me he had stayed up very late but they always say things after something has happened. One thing I knew; that he was worrying about the fight and *we* were not." (My italics.)

Long after publication of the articles, Hemingway confessed that he had not treated Dominguín fairly and half-apologized, but the damage had been done. This book stands as an unwarranted attack on Dominguín, who was not as outclassed in that long duel as Hemingway claims.

The articles had not been in circulation long when rumors began to reach us that *Life* considered their publication a disaster. Readers were impatient with the long digressions that not even Hotchner's careful editing could eliminate. The newness that had greeted *Death in the Afternoon* was replaced by a jadedness which caused readers to mutter: "We've read all this before." We were assured, erroneously it turned out, that *Life* had actually halted the series in midflight because the reception had been so negative, and we heard other reports, accurate we found later, that Hemingway himself was disgusted with the whole affair, for he realized belatedly that he had made a mistake in doubling back in the first place and in writing so copiously in the second. Representatives from *Life* admitted that they were not entirely happy with the way it had turned out. The text did not appear in book form, and Hemingway was understood to be happy when the matter died an unlamented death. An aficionado from Bar Choko said: "This time it was death in September."

My own judgment, then and now, was that Hemingway was unwise to have attempted this return to his youth; that he tried to hang far too much on the slender, esoteric thread of one series of bullfights; but that he produced a manuscript that revealed a great deal about a major figure of American literature. It is a record worth having.

To the lover of taurine literature, Hemingway's description of the historic Málaga corrida of 14 August 1959 in Chapter 11 is one of the most evocative and exact summaries of a corrida ever penned. It is a masterpiece. That afternoon the brothers-in-law fought an exceptional set of Domecq bulls, and the fame of the corrida still reverberates, because the two men cut ten ears, four tails, and two hooves. There had never before been such a performance in an arena of category.

Hemingway could have ended his manuscript on that high note, but because he was an artist who loved both the drama and the twists and turns of the arena, he ended his series with a corrida of much different quality, and on its tragiheroic note he ended what he had to say about the two men whose footsteps he had dogged like a starstruck little boy.

To those, and they are legion and of good sense, who will protest that Hemingway should have wasted so much attention on a brutal affair like bullfighting, or that a major publisher should resuscitate his essay, or that I am defending the work, I can only say that many Americans, Englishmen, and Europeans generally have found in the bullfight something worthy of attention. That one of our premier artists chose to elucidate it both in his youth and in his older age is worthy of note, and I have never been ashamed to follow in his steps.

Bullfighting is far less barbarous than American boxing, and the death of men comes far less often, in recent years something like sixty deaths in the boxing ring to one in the bull ring. And few Americans are aware that our football, high school and college, kills a shockingly higher number of young men than bullfighting and makes paraplegics of scores of others.

Of course, bullfighting has elements of brutality, but so does surgery, hunting, and the income tax. *The Dangerous Summer* is an account of the brutal, wonderful, challenging things that happened during one temporada in Spain.

The Setting

Since *The Dangerous Summer* focuses on bullfighting and its participants, both in the ring and in the stands, it is essential that the reader understand and perhaps even try to appreciate the marvelous rituals governing this art form, this elaborately choreographed dance of death. Certain definitions will be helpful.

Temporada, the season. Roughly, from late March through early October. The word embraces all the fights in all the arenas of Spain, but there are also temporadas (spanning different months) in Mexico and Peru, for example. This book deals with the exciting Spanish temporada of 1959.

Corrida, literally the running. Specifically, a complete afternoon of fights, usually with three matadors, each killing two bulls.

Plaza de toros, the bull ring. Most towns in Spain have something which passes as a plaza de toros, sometimes consisting merely of a square lined by carts. Madrid's is the premier in the world, and precedence among matadors is determined by when the man first fought as a full matador in Madrid. Sevilla's majestic plaza is the most beautiful and second in rank. Mexico City's is by far the biggest, Ronda's the most ancient and beautiful but very small, and Bilbao's the one where the fans are the toughest and bulls the biggest.

Mano a mano, hand-to-hand. A duel between two established matadors, each with great cartel, who occupy the arena alone, each killing three bulls. The rivalry can be intense, especially if there is bad blood between the two men.

Cartel, literally poster, but by extension reputation in bullfight circles, as "I have terrific cartel in Barcelona," an exact analogy to the old-time American vaudeville boast: "They loved me in Omaha." The protagonists of this book had enormous and equal cartel.

Aficionado, one who has affection for. Said especially of those who love bullfighting. Hemingway was revered in Spain as a true aficionado and a learned one.

La prensa, the press. Beyond compare, the taurine press in Spain is the most corrupt in the world. It is lively, colorful, adulatory, and for sale with a favorable judgment to any matador who can come up with three dollars. It is quite possible to attend a fight on Sunday in which Matador Sanchez was so deplorable that the police had to be brought in to protect him, and then to read on Monday that Sanchez, "despite having been given bad bulls in the lottery, performed wonders and heard petitions and music, leaving the arena on the shoulders of his adoring fans."

The Bulls

Ganadería, bull ranch, from *ganado*, herd of cattle. Each ranch is named, carries its own reputation, and produces bulls with more or less consistent characteristics. Famous as killers are the dreadful Miuras. Concha y Sierra produced first-class fighters for many decades. Pablo

Romeros are said to be "as big as three trucks running together." In these pages Hemingway speaks well of the Palhas, but he also likes the Cobaledas. When I knew the latter they were known contemptuously as "the little doughnuts," for they were notoriously weak in the legs and fell down after even the most limited exertion.

Divisa, device to distinguish things. Each ranch has its particular colors, immediately recognized by the aficionado. As a bull from a given ranch is about to enter the arena, a small barb bearing a wisp of cloth showing his divisa is implanted in his hump, so that he comes roaring in displaying his colors.

Tienta, testing. The ganadero faces a difficult dilemma. He wants to test his young bulls to see whether they are going to be brave, but he must never do this with a cloth, because bulls learn fast, and remember. Once a bull discovered that there was no man behind the enticing cloth, he would forever after ignore the cloth and go for the man. Even the most skilled matador would last about two minutes against such a knowing adversary. So on some fine day the ganadero puts men on horseback with pics to see whether his bulls can take punishment, but an even better way to estimate this is to observe the courage of the mother cow, for it is believed that a bull acquires his courage from his mother. There is no aspect of bullfighting more exhilarating to the true aficionado than to be invited to a tienta at some famous ranch, for then he sees the cows tested by real matadors using real capes. A feast is usually spread, and as the afternoon progresses, observers in the stands are invited down to try their luck with some of the smaller cows. Often the matador in charge of the tienta will invite some pretty young girl to hold one end of the broad cape while he stands well apart holding the other. With luck, the bewildered cow dashes between them. Hemingway was invited to many tientas and fought many cows, not something to smile at, for the cows can be almost as dangerous as the bulls.

Encierro, from *cerrar*, to close. The delivery of the six bulls from the ganaderia to the ring where they will be fought. In the old days a thrilling gallop through the streets; nowadays the work of truckers.

Sorteo, lottery. The highly formalized assignment of the six bulls to the matadors who will fight them. Conducted at high noon on the day of the fight by the assistants to the matadors, who draw lots and then return to where their employers are waiting with the invariable promise: "Maestro, we got you the two best. They'll charge like they were on railroad tracks, come and go."

The Dressing

It is an almost breathless honor for an aficionado to be invited to attend, at about four in the afternoon, the solemn ritual of dressing for the fight. Starting with the skimpiest white underpants, meticulously clean because if the matador is gored around the belly or the crotch, the cloth that is driven into the wound must be antiseptic, the fighter dons the traditional uniform whose features date far back into the seventeenth century. The talk is hushed. Rituals of good luck are jealously observed.

Traje de luces, suit of lights, so named because of the shimmering sequins that adorn it. The required uniform of the torero, a heavy, beautiful, expensive suit made of brocade and silk. A peón will have one, badly worn. A full matador will have many, each a different color for different occasions. During the fight, blood from the bull, or from the horses, or from the matador himself may stain the costly traje, so that after each fight the servant of the matador cleans the suit with a toothbrush.

Capilla, chapel. All bull rings have a chapel for prefight prayer, and every matador I ever knew used it or his own private travelling chapel. No matter how blasé a matador becomes, he is aware that two of the greatest fighters who ever donned the traje de luces were killed by their bulls. A score less famous died, too, and I myself have known three who died and two others who were incapacitated for life. Even the bravest pray because usually it has been men like them who have died.

At the Arena

Patio de Caballos, court yard of the horses. Here the fighters start to assemble about half an hour prior to the start of the corrida. They talk with admirers and do some admiring themselves when young women of great beauty come to greet them. I always enjoyed this nervous, exciting time almost as much as the fight.

Cuadrilla, meeting of people. The entire group of fighters who will assist one matador: his three banderilleros and cape men, his two picadors. These, dressed in full uniform, will follow him in solemn single file when he enters the ring.

Torero, fighter of bulls. The honorable, revered name for all participants in the ring, regardless of whether the individual is a full matador with great cartel or the beginning banderillero. "I am a torero" is a statement of enormous dignity.

Matador, from *matar*, to kill. This famous word, so popular in English-speaking societies, came into use relatively late in Spain to signify the lead torero. My classical Spanish dictionary gives as its meaning only *murderer*, its current usage being then unknown. Today even Spain accepts the word, and its meaning is fixed.

Novillero, beginner. Young men aspiring to be mata-

dors undergo a rigorous apprenticeship, fighting dangerous old bulls in rural places for little or no money, hoping to attract attention. A common saying: "That bull I
fought in Los Riñones was so experienced he told me
where to stand."

Sobresaliente, standby substitute. Said of either a bull or
a man. When six bulls from a ganadería are placed in the
pens for a fight, one or two substitutes, almost always
from a different ganadería, are held in reserve in case one
of the scheduled bulls is damaged or proves cowardly.
Quite often the sobresaliente is called upon. When two
matadors fight mano a mano, the management must provide a third matador, called a sobresaliente, to take over
in case both senior men are incapacitated. This happens
occasionally. But if only one of the two seniors is
wounded sufficiently to force his withdrawal, the other
must kill all the remaining bulls. I have several times
seen in the first moments of a mano a mano the senior
matador sent to the infirmary, which meant that Number Two had to fight six bulls in a row, and on one
historic occasion I saw both senior matadors go to the
infirmary within the first five minutes. The ashen sobresaliente performed well and heard music.

Rejoneador, torero who fights on horseback using a
rejón, a long-handled lance. Popular in Portugal, where
the bull is never killed, but also a feature in Spain, where
the rejoneador, on horseback, is supposed to kill the bull
with one mighty thrust. Only rarely does this happen;
usually the man has to descend from his horse, take an
ordinary muleta and sword, and finish off the bull. Purists find the act of rejón rather boring, but the placing
of banderillas—the rider no longer holding the bridle,
and guiding the horse only with his knees—can be thrilling, especially when two banderillas only eight inches
long are placed with one hand. One of the finest rejonea-

dors was Conchita Cintrón, daughter of a Peruvian army officer trained at West Point, where he took an American wife. Conchita was so dazzling that even the most macho matadors were honored to fight in the same corrida with her.

Banderillero, one who places *banderillas*. This difficult word is misused more than almost any other. During a recent television performance of *Carmen*, the announcer cried: "Look, here come the banderillas!" They did come, of course, but carried across the forearms of the banderilleros.

Picador, one who places *pics*. A heavily protected horseman with a long, pointed lance with which he pierces the bull's neck to make the animal lower his head so that the matador can work him. In the old days, which were ending just as Hemingway started attending fights, a single picador might have five or six unprotected horses killed as he rode them. This caused such a great outcry that the Spanish government ordered the horses to be protected by heavy padding, so that deaths in the ring became far less frequent.

Management of the Fight

Presidente, president. Civil law places in his hands responsibility for the orderly progress of the fight. Often called the judge, he sits in a high box overlooking everything that occurs in the ring. He is usually assisted by some revered ex-matador who advises him on the intricacies of the fight. It is the president who determines what awards the matador will receive, if any.

Alguaciles, constables or deputies of the president. Handsomely dressed in ancient style, astride a fine horse, one or two alguaciles lead the paseo into the arena at the beginning of the corrida, then one dismounts and serves as the relayer of the president's orders. This alguacil supervises the cutting of such awards as the president authorizes, and he can more or less instruct the matadors as to their obligations.

Monosabio, wise monkey. Does not dress in traje de luces, obeys the orders of the alguacil, prods the horses of the picadors to make them approach the bull, and cleans up after the bull is killed. Several times in each temporada some monosabio is injured and occasionally one is killed.

Paseo, formal entrance of the matadors with their respective cuadrillas strung out behind them. They are led by the alguacil on his horse; at the rear come the picadors. The senior matador, by date of his alternativa (formal presentation in Madrid), marches on the left as viewed by the audience, next senior on the right, youngest man in the middle. The band plays.

Espontáneo, the spontaneous one. Every act of the bullfight is rigorously formalized except one. Occasionally—say in one corrida out of twenty—some dreaming lad, hoping for a shot at immortality, will leap unannounced into the ring and, with a red cloth hastily unwrapped from around his belly, dash right up to the bull, take it away from the matador, and give it as many passes as he can before the cuadrilla capture him and lead him away. Occasionally, about once in three years, an espontáneo will be so good that he will attract the attention of an impresario, who will sign him up for a novillada, a fight for novilleros with younger bulls.

The Fight

Capeando, working with the cape alone. At the president's signal, bugles sound, the toril gates open, and the first bull of the afternoon rushes in, kicking dust.

The oldest matador works the bull with his heavy cape, and when he has done his best, the second and third matadors in turn try their luck. This is the poetic, graceful part of the fight, enjoyed by everyone. A score of intricate passes have been named, but I shall mention only three.

Veronica, from the name of the saint who succored Christ with her kerchief as he lugged his cross to Golgotha. The matador, holding the heavy brocaded cape lined with yellow silk, deftly tempts the bull to charge the cloth, and not himself. The man must keep his feet fixed and not shuffle in fear. He must also manipulate the cape so that the bull is brought back toward the man and not allowed to run wild. A series of fine veronicas can be the apex of an artistic fight.

Chicuelina, invented by a 1920s matador, Chicuelo, whom Hemingway knew and respected. The matador holds the cape out for the bull, but as the animal charges, the man deftly pulls the cape about his own body, stepping forward as the bull roars past. It is a dancing pass, quite beautiful when well executed.

Mariposa, butterfly. The matador throws the cape behind him, holding it widespread so that the edges show left and right of his exposed body. He then tantalizes the bull by enticing him with first one portion of the cape, then the other, all the while dancing backwards in a display of exquisite grace and bravery.

Pic-ing, one of those words that cannot be spelled graciously, refers to the act of the picador, who punishes the bull by plunging his heavy lance into the large muscle on the back of its neck. In the old days, when horses were often slain while the picador rode them, he absorbed terrific punishment when the bull lunged at his prostrate body. Under today's rules, which protect the horse, the picador can still be knocked about but does not run the risks he did previously.

Quite, the leading away. One of the great acts of the bullfight. The matador, still with his heavy cape, rushes up to the bull who has been hammering away at the picador's horse and lures him off with passes that can be exquisite in their delicacy and masterful in their management of the beast. And now a nice calculation comes into play. If the bull belongs to Matador A, and he dazzles it with a series of eight or nine superb passes (this happens about once in fifteen fights), he has to make this decision: "If I allow the bull to take two more pics, as custom dictates, those two other matadors will step in and maybe show off even better than I did. So I'll end the picador bit right now and deprive them of the chance. Of course, later in the fight, when the bull isn't properly tired, I may have a devil of a time mastering him, but we'll tackle that when we come to it." He indicates to the president that he wants the picadors led away, and thus frustrates his two competitors in the day's fight. Of course, when one of them gets a good bull, they'll do the same to him.

Remate, end, conclusion. A master pass that I have seen many times but still do not believe. The matador, having finished a series of passes, wants to leave the bull in a stationary position while the man prepares for his next series. He achieves this by some twist of the wrist that twirls the end of the cape, leaving the bull totally perplexed by the fact that he can see the man but never seem to catch him. "To hell with this nonsense," the bull seems to say, and there he stands, motionless.

Banderillas, the long sticks, beautifully decorated in colored papers, with a sharp barb at the end, placed in the big muscle at the shoulder of the bull. Foreign visitors to Spain usually prefer this part of the fight, wherein some slim, graceful torero with great speed of leg, control of arm, and sharpness of eye runs in a surprising trajectory, intercepts the bull as it lunges at him, then leans far over his horns to deftly place the barbs. Sometimes matadors place their own banderillas, often to enormous applause, but most have in their cuadrilla two men who can do it better, and these latter become noted specialists. To see them work is a pleasure.

Banderillas de fuego, of fire. In the old days if a cowardly bull refused to charge, or did not become sufficiently excited by the fight, the judge would signal with a red flag, whereupon the alguacil would hand the banderillero sticks with firecrackers built in near the barbs. When the banderillas were hammered home, the crackers exploded, startling the animal, who then showed the necessary movement. During one of my first corridas, before I had learned about the trick, such banderillas were used not far from where I sat, and they scared me far more than they did the bull. Since 1950 fuegos have been outlawed. In their place black banderillas, signifying shame, are used. They have extralong barbs that arouse even the most lethargic bull.

The Heart of the Fight

Now everyone but the matador and his immediate helpers retires from the ring. The horses are gone. The lovely arabesques of the banderilleros are forgotten. The matador steps forth with a small piece of red cloth draped over a stick, invariably held in the right hand along with the sword. In the old days the sword was real, but because it was too heavy it is now often of wood. As the fight progresses, the management of cloth and sword, and their exchange from hand to hand, will become crucial.

Brindis, the toast. Before the matador begins this solemn portion of the fight, he takes a position below the president's box and asks permission to dedicate the bull to some noted aficionado or a close friend, often a lady, whom he next approaches. With muleta and wooden sword in his left hand, montilla (torero's hat) in his right, he raises the hat in honor of the person being saluted, turns his back abruptly, and tosses the hat back over his shoulder to the recipient, who holds it during the faena, returning it later. The brindis is a direct descendant of the famous cry of the gladiators: *"Ave, Caesar, morituri te salutamus."* (We who are about to die salute you.) When the montilla is returned after the fight, it is customary for the person so honored to hide in it the equivalent of a ten dollar bill.

Faena, work, labor. Everything that happens with the muleta between the retirement of the picadors and the time of the kill. Principally, of course, the linked sequence of passes made with the muleta, as in the common phrase in bullfight journals: "He was on his way to winning an ear with his marvelous faena, but he lost it because of a sloppy kill." Numerous named passes go into the building of a magisterial faena, but again I shall mention only a few.

Muleta, literally, a crutch, a support, in bullfighting the red cloth with which the bull is enticed in the final act of the fight. Much smaller than the cape and much lighter, it is the matador's sole protection, and its artistic management determines in large part the success of his fight.

Derechazo, right-hander. A matador must excel in this if he is to gain cartel, but he gets little credit for doing it. It's expected. With wooden sword and muleta in his right hand, the sword acting to spread the cloth, which is held low to the ground, the matador cites (challenges) the bull, leads him past, then flicks the far end of the muleta to fix the bull before bringing him back. Of course, quite often the bull fails to see the invitation to stay and runs off, but if a matador launches six or seven linked derechazos, keeping the bull fixed, the crowd goes wild.

Natural, with the muleta in the left hand unaided by the sword and therefore much smaller in area. The noble pass with the muleta, the one that wins trophies. It is majestic because now the matador holds the frail muleta in his left hand, sword in his right and often behind the back. This means that when the bull charges, it will pass the matador's entire, exposed body before reaching the cloth. A false move here means that the matador catches a horn in the gut. Reputations are made with the natural, and no faena is considered complete without a series or an attempted one. A chain of five or six is memorable.

Paso de pecho, pass of the chest. Any sequence of naturales must be finished off with this flashy pass in which the bull, whose last charges have been low to the ground, now roars past, head high, inches from the matador's chest. One of the immortal bullfight photographs shows the Mexican show-off, Luis Procuna, delivering his version of the pass, toes together as if in cement, body erect, not a muscle moving, a look of triumph on his face as the bull thunders past, his horn inches from Procuna's face.

Adorno, finery, garniture. When the matador is satisfied that his bull has been fixed in position, hypnotized by the last remate, the man is free to do certain astonishing things. In the *teléfono* he rests his elbow on the bull's forehead, puts his hand to his own ear, and looks off into space as if taking a phone call. Or he opens his own mouth, takes the bull's horn into it, and chews. Or he stands bolt upright, his back to the perplexed bull, his rump against the horns. Most popular is the adorno in which he kneels on one knee right in the face of the bull, his nose touching the bull's as if daring him to make a move. I do not like adornos, for they make fun of the bull, but sometimes they astound me with their daring. I'm told the matador can anticipate through the muscular movement of the animal when the hypnosis of the remate is about to wear off, but the adorno still remains a mystery to me.

Rodillas, knees. Some of the most exciting passes, with either the cape or the muleta, are those given by the matador when kneeling on either one or both knees. Such passes can start the music playing.

The Kill

Estoque, the real sword, slim and very sharp. The tired bull, his brain bewildered by his futile charges at a man who seems always to disappear at the last moment, his mighty head lowered by the pics, the banderillas, and the twisting of the muleta, is now in a physical condition in which the man has a chance to kill. Going to the barrera, he hands his mozo de estoques the ceremonial sword with which he has conducted his muleta exhibition and takes instead a carefully honed, bent-downward-at-the-end killing sword, and approaches the bull, muleta in his left hand and held very low. Not many men can do what is required next. Hemingway called it "the moment of truth," that fatal instant when a man's inescapable character takes over, revealing to the world what he really stands for. Consider the complex assembly of highly skilled things the matador must do at this moment. With his left hand he must keep the muleta low, being sure that the bull's eyes remain fixed upon it. With his right hand he must hold the sword high and position it with great accuracy. With his nervous feet he must move forward in a carefully calculated path. Then, with all parts of his body in controlled and harmonious action, he must reach boldly in over the horn, place the tip of the sword precisely right, and push down till the hand almost touches the hump. Done properly, the sword kills instantly, but this happens only once in sixty or seventy tries. More likely the sword point hits bone, or enters at the wrong angle, or misses completely. Then death in the afternoon can become a very messy business. Baseball players say: "The man who hits home runs rides the Cadillac." Bullfighters could say that the man who kills well rides one. The most deplorable fight can be rescued with a great kill.

Descabello, the act of killing a bull that is dying but still on its feet, by using a killing sword with a crossbar four and one-half inches up from the tip of the blade. The crossbar prevents the sword from going all the way in as in a normal kill, but the exposed tip is extremely sharp. Using only the right hand, the matador can with his muleta cause the bull's head to drop so that the spot where the spinal cord attaches to the skull is exposed; a quick thrust with the sword severs the spinal cord and the bull drops as if shot through the heart with a rifle. But again, most often the matador has to try three or four times and the fans in the cheap seats begin shouting: "Butcher! Butcher!"

Recibiendo, receiving. You could attend a hundred bullfights and never see a real kill recibiendo, and for the very good reason that it is so perilous that not many matadors wish to try it. In its perfect form, which I have seen several times performed by the later matadors Mondeño and El Viti, who make a profession of it, the matador does everything the ordinary killer does, but instead of rushing forward to meet the bull half-way, he stands motionless like a statue, allowing the bull to come to him, depending upon the forward thrust of the bull to drive the sword home. It is a most thrilling achievement, and fans go wild when it is done properly. Hemingway was a great devotee of the kill recibiendo, for to him it epitomized the ultimate mystery of the bullfight.

Puntillero, dagger man. It is not easy to kill a bull. Occasionally a miraculous sword thrust will topple the animal dead in his tracks. The descabello also produces immediate death by severing the spinal cord. But the average bull does not die in either of those ways. What happens is that the matador tires the bull and brings him close to death with a sword thrust that would prove vital in the end, but the bull could survive many minutes before surrendering in death. To solve this problem a puntillero stands ready with a short, very sharp dagger, and once the bull falls to his knees, this man is allowed to rush in and cut the spinal cord. He does this exactly as the matador with a descabello would have done it, with a quick, sharp thrust at the base of the skull.

Trophies

Toreros fight for money, but they also fight for honor, for trophies, and for wide popular acclaim, as these next important terms demonstrate.

Pundonor, punctiliousness. Manolete, Armillita of Mexico, and my man Domingo Ortega defined honor in the bull ring, but occasionally some battered survivor like Limeño of Sanlucar de Barrameda, who has year after year volunteered to fight the killer Miuras and the boxcar Pablo Romeros when younger men are afraid to enter the arena with them, shows the world what real pundonor is. These men keep bullfighting honorable, and Hemingway paid deference to them, as do I.

Musica, music. First and most delightful of the awards comes in the later stages of a notable faena when the band begins to play. Perhaps none of the superior awards will be granted, but the journals the next day will announce: "On his second bull he heard music," and the reader will know that he performed well.

Peticiones, petitions. If a torero has heard music, it is probable that his adherents will, at the end of that particular fight, petition the judge to award a more valued trophy. "He heard peticiones," the paper will say.

Pañuelos, handkerchiefs. The spectators petition the judge by waving white handkerchiefs, and if the judge is slow in responding, the arena can become almost white: "He saw a blizzard of pañuelos."

Vuelta al ruedo, triumphal circuit of the arena. If the judge awards a major trophy, the matador makes a complete circuit of the arena—sometimes two or three—holding aloft the trophy, but even if no award is forthcoming, a matador skilled in public relations, especially if he has a clever banderillero in his cuadrilla, can tease the public into demanding a vuelta. Then the matador, feigning modesty, goes to the center of the ring, apologizes to the president, and shrugs his shoulders as if to say: "But Sir, they demand it, and there could be trouble if I don't comply." And off he goes, with the members of his cuadrilla trailing along and whipping up emotions. I have seen a clever matador, denied by the judge, make two complete vueltas, denying passionately at every step that he was really worthy of such adulation, but . . .

Oreja, ear. I cannot find when it became the custom to award a matador an ear of the bull he killed with unusual bravery, but it is an exciting moment when the judge drops his handkerchief over the edge of his box high in the balcony to signal that his alguacil may go to the dead bull, cut off an ear and hand it to the matador, who then makes a justified circuit of the arena while the audience shouts. Occasionally, two ears will be awarded for an unusual faena and a great kill.

Rabo, tail. When I first attended fights, back in the

1930s, no tails were awarded, so far as I knew, but when I returned in the 1950s one could occasionally see a tail cut—after the two ears had been awarded, of course—and in the 1960s and 1970s I saw quite a few, unwarranted in most cases.

Pata, hoof. In recent years, on very rare occasions when a matador has performed at the very apex of his art —great chicuelinas with the cape, a chain of magisterial naturales with the muleta, and a perfect kill on the first try, perhaps recibiendo—it has been possible for him to gain two ears, the tail, and a hoof: "Todos de los trofeos."

Salir en bombros, to leave the arena through the great gate on shoulders. Occasionally the aficionados will become so enraptured with a performance that they will storm into the arena at the end of the fight, raise the matador on their shoulders, and carry him triumphantly out of the arena and either to his hotel or more likely to his waiting limousine.

Cornada, horn wound. The bull can also gain his trophies. Few matadors go through an entire temporada without being gored at least once. One day when I was swimming with some matadors I was shocked by the number of old scars they carried, and the magnitude of some in the belly and near the intestines was awesome. In the old days some of these wounds would have been fatal, but with the arrival of penicillin most can be controlled. They remain as reminders that sometimes the bull wins.

Indultado, forgiven. On occasions so rare that most aficionados, including me, have never witnessed one, a bull will prove so heroic that the public refuses to let it be killed. Sometimes the matador, with tears in his eyes, will petition the judge to save this incredible animal, who is then turned out to pasture. A famous case produced one of the finer taurine photographs: the Cobaleda

bull Civilón, indultado in Barcelona in 1936 by unani-
mous petition, is seen back in his home pasture grazing
peacefully while eight of the ganadero's little children
and their friends hold hands, half-surrounding him at a
distance of less than five yards. He is staring directly at
them but making no move.

Hemingway's essay in its present book form will be trea-
sured by two special groups of people. Devotees of
American literature who revere Hemingway, of whom
I am one, will find in these pages a confused farewell
from a great and legendary figure. We witness his curious behavior toward his wife when he adopts various
attractive young women during the feria at Pamplona.
We see the longing with which he returns to those sing-
ing woods near Roncesvalles. We come suddenly upon
his own assessment of *The Sun Also Rises:* "I've written
Pamplona once and for keeps."

Certain passages reverberate with the authentic Hemingway touch: "[We] . . . stopped at the next town where
two storks were nesting on the roof of a house where the
road made a dropping bend. The nest was half built, the
female had not laid her eggs yet and they were courting.
The male would stroke her neck with his bill and she
would look up at him with storklike devotion and then
look away and he would stroke her again. We stopped
and Mary took some photographs but the light was not
too good."

We get many insights into Hemingway's character,
his bravado, his preoccupation with death, his intoler-
ance toward inferiors, his wonderful generosity when he
identified with someone he deemed worthy of respect. In
these years he met two young American friends of mine,
John Fulton, a Philadelphia boy who aspired to be a
bullfighter, and Robert Vavra, a California lad who

wanted to be an animal photographer. Listening to their stories, he impulsively drew from his wallet a check which he signed for one hundred dollars. When they tried to thank him, all he could say was: "Buena suerte."

But he could also be miserably aggressive. When he met another friend of mine, Matt Carney, who knew more about bulls than Hemingway, he goaded the young man into agreeing to a fist fight and then withdrew before any blows were exchanged.

These pages are instructive regarding a minor brouhaha that involved his friend A. E. Hotchner. Some critics, resenting the way in which Hotchner appeared to have appropriated Hemingway, accused him of being a fancifier. One extremely harsh article that appeared in *Atlantic* magazine after the publication of Hotchner's book *Papa Hemingway* even made me begin to wonder whether Hotchner had ever known the master. This manuscript, and the photographs which appeared with the *Life* articles, prove not only that Hotchner knew Hemingway intimately but also that Hemingway trusted and relied upon him. I was glad to have this clarification.

I cherish the throwaway paragraphs in which Hemingway reminds us of the sparse way he worked and of his refusal to use commas: ". . . I went into the cage of a wolf which had been recently trapped on the place and played with him which pleased Antonio. The wolf looked healthy and the odds were all against him having hydrophobia so I figured all he can do is bite you, so why not go in and see if you can work with him. The wolf was very nice and recognized someone who liked wolves."

Most such treasurable bits have been retained, and they provide affectionate glimpses of the man and the writer. On the other hand, the purely bullfight passages have been sharply cut, so that the devout aficionado will miss details which he would have savored. Both the *Life*

editors and those responsible for the present volume d
cided—properly so, I judge—to eliminate from most
the corridas the names and work of the matadors oth
than Dominguín and Ordóñez. But someone like m
knowing the matadors thus eliminated and their hist
ries, regrets the loss of revealing paragraphs like tl
following:

There were two other matadors on the bill that afternoon. "Miguelín" a short bushy-headed local boy and
fearless clown and Juan Garcia "Mondeño" a tall,
spare, grave, boy with a serenity, calmness and controlled purity of style who fought his bulls as though
he were serving Mass in a dream. He was the best new
bullfighter I saw last year.

Miguelín was the same comic figure, but a little more
unpleasant. He treated the bulls with an insolence and
contempt they had no way of returning and he knew
enough and had good enough reflexes to spread his
bad taste and his clowning contempt for everything
that made bullfighting worth watching like some
nasty syrup over the ring. He did everything but chew
bubble gum when he passed a bull. He was a home
town boy and his neighbours loved it.

Pepé Luis's second bull was difficult and also weak in
the legs. He made excellent isolated passes with cape
and muleta and tried to get something out of the bull
then quit and gave up.

The local boy Francisco Anton "Pacorro" was justifia-
bly cautious with his first bull which was very dangerous and hooked on both sides. His feet jittered away
on purpose, at the start. Then he could not control
them and it looked for a while as though the bull
would go out alive. His townspeople were merciless
with him especially all those in the sun who, if they

could have controlled their own feet, would have been
bullfighters. . . .

On the last bull, which was good, he did everything
on his knees to control the nerves that made his feet
jump away. Once he had them under control he stood
up and worked the bull beautifully with the old and
classic passes. He went in beautifully to kill but hit
bone hard. This upset him and he went back onto both
knees to pass the bull again. The bull caught him on
the ground, tossed him high in the air and he came
down sprawled like a rag doll and obviously wounded.

He shook off the people who tried to hold him,
squared the bull with the muleta and went in to kill
in a rush. The bull came out dead from the encounter
and swayed over. They carried Pacorro into the callejón and out under the stands to the infirmary. The ears
and tail followed him into the operating room while
we were making our way out through the crowded
callejón, past where the bulls were being butchered to
the cobbled patio of the picadors' horses where the
cars were parked.

I could read reminiscences like that for hours, but I do
confess that whereas aficionados like me have lost something through the cutting, the typical reader has not.
Indeed, a plethora of such material—and there are long
pages of it left on the cutting floor—would so alienate the
general public that the manuscript would probably
never be finished by most readers if it were published
intact.

The taurine reader will want to know what happened
to the conqueror Ordóñez after his incandescent tri-
umphs during that dangerous summer of 1959. In subse-
quent years I saw him fight perhaps two dozen times and
invariably he was disgraceful. Although others saw him
fight well after 1959, the times I saw him he was pudgy

and evasive, apparently terrified of any real bull he faced. He took refuge in every ugly trick that Hemingway despised, accomplishing nothing with cape or muleta and killing with a shameful running swipe from the side.

And yet we crowded the arenas to see him, hoping in vain for one final afternoon of honest triumph. It never came. Instead we saw debacles, heard boos and whistles, ducked as cushions came showering down upon him, and watched as the police prepared to rescue him if outraged fans tried to invade the arena. Hemingway was spared these indignities. He had travelled with Ordóñez when the matador was incomparable, and it was of this greatness that he wrote.

J. A. M.
Austin, Texas
1984

THE
DANGEROUS
SUMMER

CHAPTER

1

It was strange going back to Spain again. I had never expected to be allowed to return to the country that I loved more than any other except my own and I would not return so long as any of my friends there were in jail. But in the spring of 1953 in Cuba I talked with good friends who had fought on opposing sides in the Spanish Civil War about stopping in Spain on our way to Africa and they agreed that I might honorably return to Spain if I did not recant anything that I had written and kept my mouth shut on politics. There was no question of applying for a visa. They were no longer required for American tourists.

By 1953 none of my friends were in jail and I made plans to take my wife Mary to the feria at Pamplona and then to proceed to Madrid to see the Prado and after that, if we were still at large, to continue on to Valencia for the bullfights there before getting our boat to Africa. I knew that nothing could happen to Mary since she had never been in Spain in her life and knew only the very finest people. Surely, if she ever had any trouble they would rush to her rescue.

We passed quickly through Paris and drove rapidly through France via Chartres, the Valley of the Loire, and the Bordeaux bypass to Biarritz where several people were poised waiting to join us in our passage of the frontier. We ate and drank well and set an hour to meet at our hotel at Hendaye Plage and all hit the frontier together. One of our friends had a letter from Duke Miguel Primo de Rivera, then Spanish Ambassador in London, which was supposed to be able to work wonders if I ran into difficulties. This cheered me vaguely.

It had been grim and rainy when we reached Hendaye and it was grim and cloudy in the morning so that you could not see the mountains of Spain for the heavy clouds and the mist. Our friends did not show for the rendezvous. I gave them an hour and then a half an hour more. Then we left for the frontier.

It was grim at the inspection post too. I took the four passports in to the police and the inspector studied mine at length without looking up. This is customary in Spain but never reassuring.

"Are you any relation of Hemingway the writer?" he asked, still without looking up.

"Of the same family," I answered.

He looked through the pages of the passport and then studied the photograph.

"Are you Hemingway?"

I pulled myself up to modified attention and said, "*A sus ordenes*," which means in Spanish not only at your orders but also at your disposal. I had seen it said and heard it said under many different circumstances and I hoped I had said it properly and in the right tone of voice.

Anyway he stood up, put out his hand and said, "I have read all your books and admire them very much.

Let me stamp these and see if I can help you at the customs."

So that was how we came back to Spain and it seemed too good to be true. Each time we were halted by the civil guard at the three checkpoints along the Bidassoa river I expected us to be detained or sent back to the frontier. But each time the guards examined our passports carefully and politely and waved us on cheerfully. We were an American couple, a cheerful Italian, Gianfranco Ivancich from the Veneto, and an Italian chauffeur from Udine, bound for the San Fermines at Pamplona. Gianfranco was an ex-cavalry officer who fought with Rommel and was a close and dear friend who had lived with us in Cuba while he was working there. He had brought the car up to meet us at Le Havre. The driver Adamo had ambitions of becoming an undertaker and funeral director. He has achieved them and if you ever die in Udine he is the man to handle you. No one ever asked him which side of the Spanish Civil War he fought on. For my own peace of mind on that first trip I sometimes hoped it was both. Getting to know him and appreciate his versatility which was Leonardian I believe it would be perfectly possible. He might fight on one side for his principles, on another for his country or the city of Udine, and if there were a third party he could always fight for his God or for the Lancia Company or the Funeral Directing Industry to all of whom he was equally and deeply devoted.

If you want to travel gaily, and I do, travel with good Italians. We were with two fine ones in a good well-seasoned Lancia climbing up out of the green Bidassoa valley with the chestnut trees close beside the road and the mist clearing as we climbed so I knew it would be clear after the Col de Velate when we would wind down into the high plateau of Navarre.

This is supposed to be about bullfighting but I took

little interest in bullfighting then except to wish to show it to Mary and Gianfranco. Mary had seen Manolete fight in his last appearance in Mexico. It was a windy day and he drew the two worst bulls but she had liked the corrida, which was very poor, and I knew if she liked that one she would like bullfighting. They say that if you can stay away from bullfighting for a year you can stay away from it forever. That is not true but it has some truth in it and, except for fights in Mexico, I had been away for fourteen years. A lot of that time though was like being in jail except that I was locked out; not locked in.

I had read about, and trusted friends had told me about, some of the abuses that had come into bullfighting in the years of the domination of Manolete and after. To protect the leading matadors the bulls' horns had been cut off at the points and then shaved and filed down so that they looked like real horns. But they were as tender at the point as a fingernail that has been cut to the quick and if the bull could be made to bang them against the planks of the barrera they would hurt so that he would be careful about hitting anything else with them. The same effect would be produced by hitting the iron-heavy canvas of the sheathing then used to armor the horses.

With the length of the horn shortened the bull lost his sense of distance too and the matador was in much less danger of being caught. A bull learns to use his horns on the ranch in the daily arguments, squabbles and some-times serious fights with his brothers and he is more knowledgeable and skillful with them each year. So the managers of certain star matadors, who each had their strings of lesser matadors, tried to get the bull breeders to produce what we call the half-bull or medio-toro. This is a bull as little over three years as possible so he will not know how to use his horns too well. For him not to be too strong in the legs and so irreducible by the muleta, he should not have to walk too far from his pasture to water. For him to fill out to the required weight they want him grain-fed so that he will look like a bull, weigh out like a bull and come in fast like a bull. But really he is only a half-bull and the punishment softens him and leaves him manageable and, unless the matador takes very gentle care of him, he is helpless at the end.

He can wound you or kill you any time with one chopping stroke of even a shaved horn. Many people have been wounded by shaved horns. But a bull whose horns have been altered is at least ten times as safe to work and kill as a bull with his horns intact.

The average spectator cannot detect the shaved horn since he or she has had no experience with the horns of animals and does not see the slight gray-white raspiness. They look at the tips of the horns and they see a fine shining black point and they do not know that was made by rubbing the horn and polishing it with used crankcase oil. That gives a shaved horn a better sheen than saddle soap gives your scuffed shooting boots but to a trained observer it is as easy to detect as a flaw in a diamond is to a jeweler and you can detect it from a much greater distance.

The unscrupulous managers of the time of Manolete and the years after were also often the promoters, or linked with the promoters and with certain bull breeders. Their ideal for their matadors was the half-bull and many breeders concentrated on producing him in great quantities. They bred down in size for speed, for docility and easy rage and then they grained them up for weight to give the impression of size. They did not have to worry about horns. Horns could be altered and the public seeing the miracles that could be performed with such animals—men fighting backwards; men staring at the public instead of the bull, as he passed under their armpits; men kneeling in front of the ferocious animal and putting their left elbow to the bull's ear while they pretended to speak to him on the telephone; men stroking his horn and throwing away their sword and muleta while they gazed at the public like ham actors with the bull still sick and bleeding and hypnotized—the public watching this circus business thought they were witnessing a new Golden Age of bullfighting.

If the unscrupulous managers had to accept real bulls with unaltered horns from honest breeders there was always a possibility that something could happen to the bulls in the dark passageways and the stone holding boxes of the bull ring where they are confined after being sorted out at noon the day of the corrida. So if you had seen a bull bright-eyed, fast as a cat, sound in all four legs at the apartado (or sorting out and putting the bulls in the holding boxes) and this bull should come out later weak in the hind legs, someone might have dropped a heavy sack of feed on the small of his back. Or if he wandered out into the ring like a sleepwalker and the matador could only try to work him through the bull's daze so he had an animal that was disinterested and had forgotten what his great horns were for, then someone could have prodded him with a big horse syringe loaded with barbiturates.

Of course sometimes they had to fight the real bull with unaltered horns. The best fighters could do it but they did not like it because it was too dangerous. But they all did it a certain number of times each year.

So for many reasons, especially the fact that I had grown away from spectator sports, I had lost much of my old feeling for the bullfight. But a new generation of fighters had grown up and I was anxious to see them. I had known their fathers, some of them very well, but after some of them died and others lost out to fear or other causes I had resolved never to have a bullfighter for a friend again because I suffered too much for them and with them when they could not cope with the bull from fear or the incapacity that fear brings.

That year of 1953 we stayed outside of town in Lecumberri and drove to Pamplona twenty-five miles to arrive by six-thirty each morning for the running of the bulls through the streets at seven. We located our friends at the hotel in Lecumberri and we put in the usual rough seven days. After seven days of unrelenting festivity we all knew each other fairly well and we all liked each other, or most of us did, which meant it had been a good fiesta. At the start I had thought the Earl of Dudley's gold-trimmed Rolls Royce just a touch pretentious. Now I found it charming. That was the way it was that year.

Gianfranco had joined one of the dancing and drinking cuadrillas made up of bootblacks and a few aspirant pickpockets, and his bed at Lecumberri saw little of him. He created minor history by going to sleep in the fenced-off runway through which the bulls enter the ring so he would be sure to be awake for the encierro and not miss it as he had one morning. He did not miss it. The bulls ran over him. All the members of his cuadrilla were very proud.

Adamo was in the ring each morning and wanted to be allowed to kill a bull but the management had other plans.

The weather was atrocious and Mary was soaked through at the fights and caught a heavy cold with fever that stayed with her through Madrid. The bullfights were not really good except for one historic thing. It was the first time we saw Antonio Ordóñez.

I could tell he was great from the first long slow pass

he made with the cape. It was like seeing all the great cape handlers, and there were many, alive and fighting again except that he was better. Then, with the muleta, he was perfect. He killed well and without difficulty. Watching him closely and critically I knew he would be a very great matador if nothing happened to him. I did not know then he would be great no matter what happened to him and increase in courage and passion after every grave wound.

I had known his father Cayetano years before and had written a portrait of him and an account of his fighting in *The Sun Also Rises*. Everything that is in the bull ring in that book is as it was and how he fought. All the incidents outside the ring are made up and imagined. He always knew this and never made any protests about the book.

Watching Antonio with the bull I saw that he had everything his father had in his great days. Cayetano had absolute technical perfection. He could direct his subalterns, the picadors and the banderilleros, so that the entire handling of the bull, the three stages that lead to his death, was ordered and reasoned. Antonio was very much better so that every pass that he made with the cape from the time the bull came out and every move of the picadors and the placing of each pic thrust was intelligently directed toward preparing the bull for the last act of the bullfight: his domination by the scarlet cloth of the muleta which prepares him for his death by the sword.

In modern bullfighting it is not enough that the bull be simply dominated by the muleta so that he may be killed by the sword. The matador must perform a series of classic passes before he kills, if the bull is still able to charge. In these passes the bull must pass the body of the matador within hooking range of the horn. The closer the bull passes the man at the man's invitation and direction the greater the thrill the spectator receives. The classic passes are all extremely dangerous and in them the bull must be controlled by the scarlet flannel the matador holds draped over a forty-inch stick. Many trick passes have been invented in which the man really passes the bull instead of having the bull pass him, or takes advantage of his passage, saluting him, in effect, as he passes rather than controlling and directing the moves of the bull. The most sensational of these saluting passes are done on bulls which charge on a straight line and the matador knowing there is comparatively no danger turns his back on the bull to start the pass. He could pass a street car in the same way but the public loves these tricks.

The first time I saw Antonio Ordóñez I saw that he could make all the classic passes without faking, that he knew bulls, that he could kill well if he wished to, and that he was a genius with the cape. I could see he had the three great requisites for a matador: courage, skill in his profession and grace in the presence of the danger of death. But when a mutual friend told me coming out of the ring after the fight that Antonio wanted me to come up to the Hotel Yoldi to see him I thought: Don't start being friends with bullfighters again and especially not with this one when you know how good he is and how much you will have to lose if anything happens to him.

Fortunately I have never learned to take the good advice I give myself nor the counsel of my fears. So meeting Jesús Córdoba, the Mexican bullfighter who was born in Kansas, speaks excellent English, and had dedicated a bull to me the day before, I asked him where the Yoldi was and he offered to walk over with me. Jesús Córdoba was an excellent boy and a good and intelligent matador and I enjoyed talking with him. He left me at the door of Antonio's room.

Antonio lay naked on the bed except for a hand towel

as a fig leaf. I noticed the eyes first; the darkest, brightest, merriest eyes anybody ever looked into and the mischief urchin grin, and could not help seeing the scar welts on the right thigh. Antonio reached his left hand out, the right had been badly cut by the sword on his second kill, and said, "Sit down on the bed. Tell me. Am I as good as my father?"

So looking in those strange eyes, the grin gone now along with any doubt that we were going to be friends, I told him that he was better than his father and I told him how good his father was. Then we talked about the hand. He said he would fight with it in two days. It was a deep cut but had not severed any tendon or ligament. His telephone call came through that he had put in to his fiancée, Carmen, the daughter of Dominguín his manager and the sister of Luis Miguel Dominguín the matador, and I excused myself to get out of hearing distance of the phone. When the call was finished I said good-bye. We made an appointment to meet at El Rey Noble with Mary and have been friends ever since.

When we first saw Antonio fight, Luis Miguel Dominguín had retired. We met him first at Villa Paz, the ranch he had just bought near Saelices on the road from Madrid to Valencia. I had known Miguel's father for many years. He had been a good matador at a time when there were two great matadors, and later a very able and astute businessman and he had discovered and managed Domingo Ortega. Dominguín and his wife had three sons and two daughters. All three sons had been matadors. Luis Miguel had been facile and talented in everything, was a great banderillero and what the Spanish call a torero muy largo; that is, he had an extensive repertoire of passes and elegant tricks, and could do anything with a bull and kill just as well as he wanted to.

It was Dominguín, the father, who asked us to stop and see Luis Miguel at his newly purchased ranch and have lunch on our way to Valencia. Mary, Juanito Quintana, an old friend from Pamplona who was the model for the hotel keeper Montoya in *The Sun Also Rises*, and I came to the cool, darkened house after driving through the July heat of New Castille with the hot wind from Africa blowing the chaff in the air from the threshing floors along the road. Luis Miguel was a charmer, dark, tall, no hips, just a touch too long in the neck for a bullfighter, with a grave mocking face that went from professional disdain to easy laughter. Antonio Ordóñez was there with Carmen, Luis Miguel's younger sister. She was very dark and beautiful with a lovely face and she was beautifully built. She and Antonio were engaged to be married that fall and you could see in everything they did and said how much they loved each other.

We inspected the animals, the poultry and stables and the gun room and I went into the cage of a wolf which had been recently trapped on the place and played with him which pleased Antonio. The wolf looked healthy and the odds were all against his having hydrophobia so I figured all he can do is bite you, so why not go in and see if you can work with him. The wolf was very nice and recognized someone who liked wolves.

We looked at the new-built swimming pool that was not yet filled and we admired the bronze life-size statue of Luis Miguel, a rare thing for a man to have around his own finca in his own lifetime, and I thought Miguel looked better than his statue although his statue looked just a little bit nobler. But it is hard for a man to compete with his own bronze statue in his own side yard.

The next time I saw Miguel was in Madrid in May of 1954, after we came back from Africa. He came up to our room at the Palace Hotel where everyone had come in after a particularly poor corrida on a windy, rainy, squally day. The room was full of people and glasses and smoke and too much talk about something it would be better to forget and Miguel really looked awful. When he is at his best he looks like a combination of Don Juan and a good Hamlet but that noisy evening he looked drawn, beat-up and tired.

Miguel was still retired but was thinking of taking a few fights in France and I went out in the country with him a couple of times, out toward Escorial under the lee of the Guadarramas while he trained with the young fighting cows to see how long it would take to put himself into shape to fight again. I liked to see him work and watch how hard he worked, never resting nor sparing himself and how when he began to tire or his wind to shorten he would pile it on until it was the animal who was exhausted. Then he would start working with another beast, the sweat running off him and he breathing deeply to get his wind back again as he waited for the new animal to come in. I admired his grace and his facility and his toreo or way of working with bulls which was based on his physical faculties, his wonderful legs, his reflexes, his tremendous repertoire of passes and his encyclopedic knowledge of bulls. It was a great pleasure to see him work out there and the country was beautiful in the spring now that the rains had stopped. There was only one trouble for me. His style did not move me at all.

I did not like the way he handled a cape. By good luck I had seen all the great cape handlers since modern bullfighting began with Belmonte and even in the country I could tell that Luis Miguel was not among them. That was only a detail though and I enjoyed his company greatly. He had a mocking humor and was very cynical and I learned much from him about many things when we had the good luck to have him stay with us at the Finca in Cuba for a while. We had long talks each day down at the pool after I would finish work. At the time Luis Miguel had no intention of returning to the bulls. He was unmarried and playing the field and one day he would think of being one thing and on another something else. He used to go out nights with Agustín de Foxa the Spanish poet who was serving as a secretary at the Spanish Embassy. Agustín enjoyed life very much and during his Foxa period, when Luis Miguel and our chauffeur Juan would get back to the Finca shortly before or after daylight, Miguel thought seriously of taking up the diplomatic life.

He also thought about taking up writing. If Ernesto could write, I think he reasoned, it must be easy. I explained there was nothing to it if you did it right and told him how I did it. So for a couple days we each wrote in the mornings and he brought what he wrote down to the pool at noon.

Miguel was a wonderful companion, a perfect guest and he told me some of the damndest things I have ever heard both about life and about bullfighting.

That was one of the things that made the 1959 campaign so terrible. If Luis Miguel had been an enemy and not my friend and Carmen's brother and Antonio's brother-in-law it would have been easy. Not easy, perhaps, but you would not have cared except as a human being.

2

FROM THE END OF JUNE IN 1954 UNTIL AUGUST 1956 WE
were in Cuba working. I was in bad shape with a back
that had been broken in plane crashes in Africa and I was
trying to get well again. Nobody was sure how the back
would turn out until we had to test it off Cabo Blanco,
Peru, fishing for a very big marlin for the film of *The Old
Man and the Sea.* It stood up all right and when our work
on that picture was finished for better or for worse we
spent the month of August in New York.

We sailed from New York on September first, plan-
ning to go to Spain from Paris to see Antonio fight at
Logroño and Zaragoza and then go on out to Africa
where we had unfinished business.

We landed at Le Havre in a shambles of reporters and
camera people of all sexes and found Mario Casamassima
with a new old Lancia. He had been sent down from
Udine by Gianfranco to replace Adamo who had become
such a big man in the funeral world in Udine and vicin-

ity that he could no more leave his clients than could a popular obstetrician.

He felt heartbroken, he wrote, not to come so that we might share Spain again together but he knew we would find Mario worthy of his native city which has the highest per capita ownership of Lancias of any city in the world. He was a racing driver, a beginning TV director, and he could load the top of the Lancia like a pack mule, lash it down, and with that built-in headwind pass every product that Mercedes put on the road. He was also what the French call *debrouillard*, which means if he got into it he could get out of it and if you wanted it he could get it not just wholesale but on loan from a new-found and devoted friend. He made these friends every night and in all garages and hotels. He did not know any Spanish but he got along all right.

We got to Logroño just in time to see the corrida. It was a very fine one. The bulls were brave, big, fast and untampered with and the matadors worked close, closer, and the very closest possible and each one did everything that he could do.

Antonio almost made me choke up with the cape. Not the kind of choking where people sob like the classic picture of the Frenchman at the Fall of France but the kind where your chest and throat tighten up and your eyes dim seeing something that you thought was dead and done with come to life before you. It was being done more purely, more beautifully and closer and more dangerously than it could be done and he was controlling the danger and measuring it exactly to a micrometric proportion. All this time he was controlling a half-ton of charging animal with a deadly weapon on each side of his head, with a percale cape passing him back and forth past his waist and knees and making sculpture with him that in the relationship of the two figures and the slow, guiding movement of the cape that merged them was as beautiful as any sculpture I had ever seen.

When he had finished the first series of veronicas, Rupert Belville, our English friend and decades long an aficionado, Juanito Quintana, and I looked at each other and shook our heads. There was nothing that we could say. Mary held my hand tightly.

Now the first one was over and he would do whatever best suited the bull and what he thought was best and make a great faena and then he would kill him to please me. He loves secrets and I did not know this one then. The secret was that he was killing recibiendo which is provoking the charge by moving the left knee forward and swinging the muleta forward and as the bull charges waiting him out and as his head lowers, uncovering the slot between his shoulder blades, shoving the sword in from the palm of the hand with a straight wrist, leaning in after it so that the man and bull become one figure as the sword goes in until they are joined and the left hand, all this time, is keeping the bull's head down with the muleta low, low, and guiding him out of the encounter. It is the most beautiful way to kill and the bull has to be prepared for it all through the faena. It is also the most dangerous since, if the bull is not perfectly controlled by the left hand and raises his head, the horn wound will come in the chest. Antonio was killing bulls recibiendo that fall of 1956 for his own pleasure, to show the public what he could do, for pride in doing something the others could not or would not do and to please me.

I did not know this until the end of the season when he dedicated a bull to me in these words, "Ernesto, you and I know that this animal is worthless but let's see if I can kill him the way you like it."

He did. But before the end of the season Dr. Tamames

who was his and Luis Miguel's private surgeon and old friend said to me, "If you have any influence with him tell him not to overwork that stuff. You know where the cornada comes and I'm his surgeon."

After the last corrida at Zaragoza I was disgusted and decided I was through with the bulls for a while. I knew Antonio could deal with any bulls and could be one of the greatest matadors of all time and I did not want his place in history to be denied him or to be fouled up by the maneuvers that were going on. I knew present-day bullfighting, the modern manner of working, was much more dangerous and infinitely closer and better done than the old days and I knew they needed the half-bull to do it. That was all right with me. Let them have the half-bull as long as he was big enough to be respectable and not a novillo or admitted three-year-old, and as long as his horns were intact and he was not tampered with. But some of the time and in certain cities he would have to fight real bulls and I knew he could do it and could handle them as well as the very greatest fighters.

Luis Miguel had married a charming wife and come out of retirement. He was fighting in France though and in North Africa. In France the bulls' horns were all shaved I was informed and I had no interest in going up there. I decided to wait to see Miguel fight until he would be fighting in Spain.

So we went back to Cuba and worked all 1957 and all 1958 either in Cuba or in Ketchum, Idaho. Mary took wonderful care of me through a long bad time and working hard and with plenty of exercise I got healthy and sound again.

Antonio had a great year in 1958. We were nearly ready to go over twice but I could not interrupt my work on the novel I was writing.

We sent a Christmas card to Antonio and Carmen and I told Antonio we had missed the 1958 season but that we would not miss 1959 no matter what and would get over in time for the feria of San Isidro the middle of May in Madrid.

When the time came I hated to leave America and I hated to leave Cuba when we got there. The Gulf Stream was just moving in toward shore and the big, black-winged flying fish were starting to show the last day I came down the coast to Havana with the *Pilar* before we flew to New York to get the boat for Algeciras. I hated to miss a spring out of my life on the Gulf Stream but I had given my word at Christmas that I would come to Spain. I had made the reservation that if the bullfights were fixed or phony I would leave and go back to Cuba explaining to Antonio why I could not stay. I would not say anything to anyone else about it and I knew he would understand. The way it turned out I would not have missed the spring, summer and fall for anything else that you could do. It would have been tragic to miss it and it was tragic to watch it. But it was not a thing that you could miss.

CHAPTER

3

THE VOYAGE ON THE *CONSTITUTION* COMMENCED WITH FAIR and sunny weather that lasted for a day, then we ran into nasty weather with rain, overcast and heavy following and quartering seas and stayed in it almost to the Strait of Gibraltar. The *Constitution* was a large and pleasant ship and there were many nice and friendly people on board. We called her the "Constitution Hilton" since she seemed the least nautical means of transportation either of us had ever travelled in. Perhaps the "Sheraton-Constitution" would have been better but we can call her that another time. Compared to travelling on the old *Normandie,* the *Île de France* or the *Liberté,* it was like living at any good Hilton hotel rather than having your apartment at the Paris Ritz on the garden side.

After landing at Algeciras we drove to the home of the Davis family, Bill and Annie and their two small children, in the hills above Málaga in a villa called La Consula. There was a gate with a man on guard when it was not locked. There was a long gravelled driveway bordered by cypresses. There was a forested garden as lovely as the Botánico in Madrid. There was a wonderful huge cool house with big rooms and *esparto* grass reed-plaited mats in the corridors and the rooms and every room was full of books and there were old maps on the walls and good pictures. There were fireplaces for when it would be cold.

There was a swimming pool fed by water from a mountain spring and there was no telephone. You could go barefoot but it was cool in May and moccasins were better for the marble stairs. You ate wonderfully and drank well. Everyone let everyone else alone and when I would wake in the morning and go out on the long balcony that ran around the second floor of the house and look out over the pines in the garden to the mountains and the sea and listen to the wind in the pines I knew I had never been in a finer place. It was a wonderful place to work and I started working at once.

It was the end of the spring bullfighting season in Andalucía. The feria of Sevilla was over. Luis Miguel had been scheduled to fight his first fight in Spain of the season at Jerez de la Frontera on the day the *Constitution* had landed in Algeciras but had sent in a medical certificate that he could not appear due to an attack of ptomaine poisoning. None of this sounded too good and I thought the best thing might be to stay on at the Consula and work and swim and see the occasional fight when they were in convenient range. But I had promised Antonio to meet him at Madrid for the San Isidro fights and I had to get the remaining material I needed to finish an appendix for *Death in the Afternoon.*

Everyone had expected us at Jerez when Antonio fought there on May third, according to Rupert Belville who turned up at the Consula after the fight driving a gray beetle-shaped Volkswagen that fitted his six feet four closer than the cockpit of a fighter plane. Antonio had told them, "Ernesto has to work and I have to work. We are meeting in Madrid in the middle of the month." Juanito Quintana was with Rupert and I asked him how Antonio was.

"He's better than ever," Juanito said. "He is more confident and absolutely secure. He's crowding the bull all of the time. Wait till you see him."

"Did you see anything wrong?"

"No. Nothing."

"How is he killing?"

"He goes in high, crossing perfectly, with the muleta way down the first time. If he hits bone the first time then the second time he goes in he drops the sword just a touch. It's not low. It's just a touch off so he reaches the artery. He's learned the spot where it is still high and he goes in just the way he should and takes all the chances; but he's learned how to miss the bone."

"Do you still think we were right about him?"

"Yes, hombre, yes. He's just as good as we thought he was and the punishment he's taken has strengthened him. It hasn't diminished him at all in any way."

"And how is Luis Miguel?"

"Ernesto, I don't know how it will be. Last year in Vitoria he had a corrida of real bulls, Miuras, but not the old ones of our time. Good ones but real bulls and he couldn't deal with them. They dominated him and he's a dominator."

"Has he been fighting anything where they haven't fooled with the horns?"

"Maybe. A few. Certainly not many."

"Is he in good shape?"

"They say he is in wonderful shape."

"He'll need to be."

"Yes," Juanito said. "Antonio is a lion. He's had eleven bad wounds now and after each one he's better."

"He runs about one a year," I said.

"Always one a year," Juanito said.

I knocked three times on the trunk of the big pine tree we were standing by in the garden. The wind was blowing hard through the tops of the trees and on bullfight days it stayed with us all spring and all the summer. I never knew as windy a summer in Spain and no one remembered as many bad gorings and horn wounds in a season.

For me the great number of matadors wounded and rewounded badly in 1959 was due first to the wind which can uncover and expose the man when he is handling cape or muleta and leave him at the mercy of the bull, second to the fact that all other matadors were competing against Antonio Ordóñez and trying to do what he could do, wind or no wind.

Bullfighting is worthless without rivalry. But with two great bullfighters it becomes a deadly rivalry. Because when one does something, and can do it regularly, that no one else can do and it is not a trick but a deadly dangerous performance only made possible by perfect nerves, judgment, courage and art and this one increases its deadliness steadily, then the other, if he has any temporary failure of nerves or of judgment, will be gravely wounded or killed if he tries to equal or surpass it. He will have to resort to tricks and when the public learns to tell the tricks from the true thing he will be beaten in the rivalry and he will be very lucky if he is still alive or in business.

Juanito Quintana and I had known each other for thirty-four years and we had not seen each other for two so we had much to talk about walking in the garden that morning. We talked of what was wrong with the bullfights and what was being done to remedy the abuses and what remedies we thought would work and which ones we thought were impractical. We had both seen bullfighting almost destroyed by abuses, by the picadors bleeding the bull half dead, putting the cutting steel of the pic into the same hole and twisting and turning it, pic-ing into the spinal column, into the ribs, any place they could destroy the bull rather than try to pic him properly to tire him and steady him and bring his neck down so he would be able to be killed properly. We both knew that any fault the picador commits is the fault of his matador, or if the matador is young and without authority, the fault of the confidential banderillero or the manager. Nearly every abuse committed in bullfighting is the fault of the manager but if the matador did not agree to it he could protest it.

We discussed Luis Miguel and Antonio being managed by Luis Miguel's two brothers, Domingo and Pepé Dominguín. We agreed that it was a very difficult money situation as Luis Miguel would consider himself a bigger draw at the gate than Antonio due to his longer fame and service and Antonio would consider very strongly that he was a better matador than Miguel and would be out to show it every time. It looked very hard on family life and very good for bullfighting. It also looked very dangerous.

The first twelve days of May went very fast. I worked early then swam around noon for fun, but with discipline to keep in shape; we all lunched late, perhaps went into town for the late mail and papers and to the Boîte, a night spot out of Simenon at the big Miramar Hotel on the sea in the center of Málaga where we had come to know the people who were working there and then back to the hills to dine very late at the Consula. On the thirteenth of May we started for Madrid and the bullfights.

Starting out to drive in a part of the country you do not know, the distances all seem longer than they are, the difficult parts of the road much worse than it is, the dangerous curves more dangerous and the steep ascents have a greater percentage of grade. It is like going back into your childhood or early youth. But the drive from Málaga on the sea up into and over the coastal range of mountains is rugged even when you get to know every curve and every advantage you can take. On this first trip from Málaga to Granada to Jaen with a driver who had been recommended to Bill it was appalling. He was wrong on every turn. He relied on the horn to protect him against down-coming overloaded trucks that could do nothing to save him if he was wrong and he chilled me and spooked me hollow both climbing and descending. I tried to watch the valleys and small stone towns and farms spread out below us as we climbed and looked back at the broken ranges running to the sea. I looked at the naked dark trunks of the cork oaks where the bark had been cut and stripped a month before and I looked down into the deep crevasses on a turn and at the fields of gorse with limestone jutting out that rolled away to the high stone peaks and took the stupid driving as it came only trying to keep it from being suicidal by quiet suggestions or orders regarding speed or passing.

In Jaen the driver nearly hit a man in the street, driving too fast with no regard for pedestrians. That made him more amenable to suggestion and since we had a good road now we pushed on and crossed the valley of the Guadalquivir at Bailén and worked up into another plateau and into mountain country again, with the Sierra Morena dark on our left. We passed the high rolling hills of the Navas de Tolosa where the Christian kings of Castille, Aragon and Navarre defeated the Moors. It was good country for a battle, either to defend or to attack, once the pass had been forced and it was strange to roll through it and think what it would have cost to move through the same terrain on July sixteenth of 1212 and what these same bare mountain meadows must have looked like on that day.

Then we climbed steeply and with many turns up through the pass of Despenaperros which separates Andalucia from Castille. Andalucians say no good bullfighter has ever been born north of this pass. The road is well built and safe for any good driver and at the top there are several roadhouse eating places and inns that we were to get to know well that summer. But on this day we pressed on down the pass, the road easy now, but stopped at the next town where two storks were nesting on the roof of a house where the road made a dropping bend. The nest was half built, the female had not laid her eggs yet and they were courting. The male would stroke her neck with his bill and she would look up at him with storklike devotion and then look away and he would stroke her again. We stopped and Mary took some pictures but the light was not too good.

As we came down into the flat wine country of Valdepenas the vines were hardly hand-high and the great acreage of them swept smooth away to the dark hills. We drove on the good new road through the wine country and watched for partridges to come to dust by the side of the wagon road that paralleled the highway and we stopped for the night at the Government Inn, or Parador, in Manzanares. It was only a hundred and seventy-four kilometers to Madrid, but we wanted to drive the country in daylight and the bullfight was not until six o'clock the next afternoon.

Early in the morning before anyone was up at the inn
Bill Davis and I walked three kilometers down a side
road into the center of the old La Mancha town past the
squat, white-washed bull ring where Ignacio Sánchez
Mejías was fatally wounded and through narrow streets
to the Cathedral Square and then followed the back trail
of the black-clad early morning shoppers coming from
the market. It was a clean, well-run market and there was
plenty to buy but many of the shoppers were bitter
about the prices; especially of the fish and meat. After
Málaga, where I did not know the dialect, it was wonderful to hear the clear, beautiful Spanish and understand
everything that was being said.

We had coffee and milk and dipped good bread in it for
breakfast in a tavern and drank a few double shot glasses
of the draft wine and ate a few slices of Manchegan
cheese. The new high road had bypassed the town and
the man at the bar told us very few travellers stopped at
taverns now.

"This town is dead," he said, "except on market days."

"How will the wine be this year?"

"It's too early to know anything," he told me. "You
know as much as I do. It's always good and always the
same. The vines grow like weeds."

"I like it very much."

"So do I," he said. "That's why I speak badly of it. You
never speak badly of anything you don't like. Not now."

We walked fast to the inn. It was an upgrade and good
exercise and the town behind us was sad and easy to
leave.

When we had loaded the baggage and were starting
out the court yard to the road that led to the highway the
driver crossed himself fervently.

"Anything wrong?" I asked. He had made the sign of
the cross once before when we were driving the first

night from Algeciras to Málaga and I had thought we must be passing a spot where something terrible had happened and had been silently respectful. But this was on a good morning leaving on a fine make-time road for a short run to the capital and I knew from his conversation that the driver was not overly devout.

"No, nothing," he said. "Only that we should reach Madrid safely."

I didn't hire you to drive by miracles, I thought, nor exclusively by divine intervention. The driver should contribute a certain amount of métier and confidence and check his rubber carefully before inviting God to be his co-pilot. Then I thought again and remembering the women and children involved and the necessity for solidarity in this passing world I repeated his gesture. Then, to justify this perhaps excessive preoccupation with our own safety which seemed premature if we were to spend three months, days and nights, on the roads of Spain, and selfish if we were to spend that time with bullfighters, I prayed for all those I had in hock to Fortune, for all friends with cancer, for all girls, living and dead, and that Antonio would have good bulls that afternoon. He did not but on the other hand we reached Madrid safely after a jeopardous ride through La Mancha and the steppes of New Castille and the driver was returned, without prejudice, to Málaga when we discovered, outside the entry of the Hotel Suecia, that he did not know how to park a car in the city. Bill Davis parked it for him finally and took over the driving for the rest of the year.

The Suecia was a pleasant new hotel behind the old Cortes in walking range of the old Madrid. From Rupert Belville and Juanito Quintana, who had come up ahead of us, we found Antonio had spent the night at the Hotel Wellington out in the new fashionable quarter where most of the new hotels are. He wanted to sleep and to dress away from home to avoid having the journalists, admirers, followers and promoters in the house. The Wellington, too, was not too far from the bull ring and with the traffic as it is on San Isidro days that trip should be as short as possible. Antonio likes to be at the ring with time to spare and being jammed in traffic is bad for everyone's nerves. It is the worst preparation for the fight.

The hotel suite was full of people. Some I knew. Most I did not. There was an inner circle of followers in the salon. Most of them middle-aged. Two were young. All were very solemn. There were many people having to do with the business of bullfighting and several reporters, two from French illustrated magazines with photographers. The only people who were not solemn were Cayetano, Antonio's oldest brother, and Miguelillo, his sword handler.

Cayetano wanted to know if I still had my silver vodka flask.

"Yes," I said. "For emergencies."

"This is an emergency, Ernesto," he said. "Let's step out into the corridor."

We stepped out, saluted each other's health and then stepped back in again and I went in to see Antonio. He was dressing.

He looked the same as ever except that he was a little more mature and very dark from the ranch life. He was neither nervous nor solemn. He was going to bullfight in an hour and fifteen minutes and he knew exactly what that meant and what he must do and what he was going to do. We were very happy to see each other and whatever we shared was there exactly as it had been.

I like to get out of a dressing room fast, so after he had asked about Mary and I had asked about Carmen and he had said we would all eat together that night I said, "I'll leave you now."

"Will you come by afterwards?"

"Sure," I said.

"Till then," he said and smiled the bad boy smile that came naturally and easily and unforced even before the first fight of the season in Madrid. He was thinking about the bullfight but he was not worried.

It was a bad bullfight and the ring was packed. The bulls were hesitant and dangerous, half-charging and stopping in the middle of their charge. They were hesitant in going in on the horses. They were overfed on grain and were overweight for their size and those that did charge the horses at all well weakened in their hind legs and ran out of gas.

Victoriano Valencia who was confirming his alternativa as a full matador in Madrid showed that he was no more than an apprentice still with a few brilliant performances behind him and no sure future. Julio Aparicio, a complete and skillful matador, conducted the lidia, the working and the placing of his bulls, stupidly. He did nothing to eliminate their defects and spent his time showing the public that they would not charge rather than in making them charge. He was suffering from that defect of the matador who has made much money early in his career and now waits for a bull without difficulties or danger rather than getting from each bull whatever that bull can give. Aparicio did nothing of value with either of his bulls but he stuck them ably and promptly and with no style to prove to anyone who cared, and to himself, that he could do something efficiently. No one cared.

Antonio saved the corrida from being a disaster and gave Madrid the first view of what he had become. His first bull was worthless. He was hesitant with the horses and did not want to charge frankly but Antonio picked him up with the cape delicately and suavely, fixed him, taught him, encouraged him by letting him pass closer and closer. He fabricated him into a fighting bull before your eyes. Antonio in his own enjoyment and knowledge of the bull seemed to be working in the bull's head until the bull understood what was wanted of him. If the bull had a worthless idea Antonio would change it for him subtly and firmly.

Since I had seen him he had refined the artistry of his cape work until it was perfection. It was not simply beautiful passes made on the round trip passage of the ideal straight charging bull that all matadors hope for. Each pass controlled and directed the bull and passed him his full length past the man controlling him with the folds of the cape and then turning him and bringing him back again, always bringing the horns within centimeters of the man and the cape moving ahead so suavely and tempered in its movement it was like slow motion in a picture or a dream.

With the muleta he used no tricks. The bull was his now. He had made him and perfected him and convinced him without ever hurting him or twisting him or punishing him. He cited him from in front with the muleta in the left hand and passed the bull by him and around him again and again, then brought his horns and his whole bulk by his chest with the real pase de pecho and with a turn of his wrist set him squared off facing for the kill.

He went in once, sighting carefully high up between the tops of the shoulder blades for the kill, and hit bone, and bumped out over the horns. The second time he sighted for the same spot and the sword went in to the cross guard below the pommel. By the time Antonio's fingers were blooded the bull was dead but the bull did not know it for a while. Antonio watched him with his hand up, guiding his death as he had guided his one performance in his short life, and suddenly the bull shuddered and crashed over.

His second bull came out strong but used himself up on the horses and started to break off and brake with his hind feet in the center of his charges. He was bad on both sides and hooked irrationally with both his left and his right horn but especially with his right. There was no plan in the way he defended himself. He was nervous, hysterical and did not straighten out no matter where Antonio took him and worked on him. Different bulls will become confident in different parts of the ring but although Antonio worked close and low and rhythmically with him and then punished him with low passes turning him on himself to try to take possession of him and stop the half-charges and random hooking and trotting, the bull stayed half-cowardly and hysterical. You could not do a modern type of faena with him without going to the hospital. Since bullfighting started there has only been one thing to do with this particular trotting type of bull; get rid of him promptly. So Antonio did it.

Afterwards sitting on the bed up in the room at the Wellington while he cooled out after the shower, Antonio said, "Contento Ernesto with the first one?"

"You know," I said. "Everybody knew. You had to make him. You had to invent him."

"Yes," he said. "But he turned out pretty well."

That night, eating at the Coto, an indoor and outdoor restaurant with a tree-shaded garden close to the old Ritz and opposite the Prado Museum, we were all very jolly because Antonio had been great in his first bull, he did not have to fight the next day, which is the ideal length of time between fights, there was stuff in the corrals that looked wonderful and no one knew that the weather would be foul. There was our outfit and Dr. Manolo Tamames, who is Antonio's and Luis Miguel's personal surgeon and great friend, and his wife, a couple of bull breeders, and Antonio and Carmen. It was good to be together again and we talked and joked about many things. Like all truly brave people Antonio is light-hearted and likes to joke and make fun of serious things. Once when he was making fun of someone and pretending to a complete goodness I said to him, "You're so noble and good. What about what you did to your great friend today?"

He and Aparicio were very good friends. In one of the bulls of this first afternoon of the feria Aparicio had been busy showing the public that it was impossible to do anything with the cape on the bull he had drawn. On the next quite Antonio took the bull away from the horse and did six beautiful, slow-tempered, endless veronicas on Aparicio's bull which absolutely destroyed his friend's day and showed the public how the bull could be handled if the bullfighter wanted to go to him and spend a little of his chances of life on him.

"I told him I was sorry," Antonio said.

Luis Miguel had fought his first fight in Spain at Oviedo in Asturias on May seventh and had cut the ears of both his bulls. He had fought his second corrida at Talavera de la Reina on May sixteenth, the same day Antonio had fought weak Pablo Romero bulls in Madrid. In Talavera Luis Miguel had fought Salamanca bulls and had a great triumph cutting both ears and the tail of his first bull and both ears of his second. Luis Miguel had been in wonderful condition and was fighting in two days in Barcelona. They had not filled the ring in the Talavera fight.

In addition to his two fights in Spain, Luis Miguel had fought three times in France so far; at Arles, Toulouse and Marseilles. His work had been brilliant. My informants said that in all of these fights the bulls' horns had been fixed in varying degrees. He was going to fight on the next day in Nimes and Antonio would fight on the following day in that same great Roman arena. I love Nimes but did not feel like leaving Madrid, where we had just arrived, to make such a long trip to see bulls with altered horns fought so decided to stay in Madrid.

Sooner or later Antonio and Luis Miguel would have to fight together in open competition because the economics of bullfighting were in bad shape with the hoggish prices the managers demanded and only these two could fill the rings at such prices. Knowing them both and knowing Antonio better and knowing now how much less he would be getting than Luis Miguel, I knew it would be deadly.

Antonio came back from France where he and Luis Miguel had both triumphed on successive days. Luis Miguel had cut one ear of the second of his two bulls on the seventeenth at Nimes and on the eighteenth Antonio had cut an ear of each of his bulls and both ears and tail of the final bull that he had fought and killed in substitution for El Trianero who had been tossed and taken a three-inch wound in his left arm attempting a pass on his knees with the cape as the bull came into the ring.

The public had been wild about Antonio in a part of the country where Luis Miguel had a tremendous following and had always been considered the number one bullfighter and the rivalry between Antonio and Luis Miguel was now launched on an international basis with photographers and reporters from French and other European illustrated papers arriving in Madrid to see his next fight.

4

MARY HAD A REALLY BAD COLD THAT SHE HAD CAUGHT ONE day we had been rained out after the third bull during the San Isidro feria in Madrid. She had tried to get rid of it but the feria had been too mixed up and the hours too crazy and the fights starting so late had given the small wind that comes down from the Sierras that they say will kill a man but not blow out a candle too many chances at her. She tried resting and getting to bed early and we ate in bed a couple of times and she thought she was in shape to make the drive to Córdoba on May twenty-fifth. Rupert Belville had left his Volkswagen when he went back to London and wanted us to take it down to Málaga, so Bill Davis and I in the English Ford and Mary and Annie Davis in the smaller car drove fast to Córdoba seeing the same country of Castille and La Mancha we had driven through and noticing how much the vines had grown and how the early wheat had been damaged and flattened by the storms that had spoiled the feria.

Córdoba is a cattle town as well as many other things and the crowd at the Palace Hotel was gay, hearty and cheerful. The hotel was full. Mary and Annie got in a little later than we did and a friend gave Mary his room to lie down and rest in until time to go to the fight.

It was a strange bullfight. Pepé Luis Vásquez who had been an excellent bullfighter with a very delicate style had come out of retirement to fight enough fights to buy a large property he wanted. He was a fine man and a loyal companion to other bullfighters but being away from the bulls for so long his reflexes were poor and he could not dominate his nerves if the bull had any difficulties that made him dangerous. He had put on weight in retirement and the delicacies and embroideries of his style now, with his plumpness and the lack of any light-hearted quality in his work, seemed sad and pitiful and he was unable to conceal his fear. He was very poor in two bulls.

Jaime Ostos, a boy from Ecija, a lovely white town to the west of Córdoba on the way to Sevilla, was as brave as the wild boar of the Sierras of his country. Like the wild boar he was almost insanely brave when angry or wounded and he seemed still punchy from a concussion he had received in his last fight with Luis Miguel at Barcelona. I liked him and I was worried sick by him all afternoon as he steadily increased the danger until it seemed semi-suicidal. I knew he was fighting in front of his home town people and that there had been a row at the start of the season and he had said he would not fight on the same card with Antonio. Taking all this into account he still seemed like an absolute bet not to live out the season. But except for minor gorings he got away with it all year. On that day in Córdoba his white and silver suit was covered with the bull's blood from passing him so close. No one ever truly asked the bull to kill him and then thwarted him by sheer luck, bravery, and reckless skill more times than Jaime Ostos did. He cut both ears of his first bull and would have cut ears on the second but for the bad luck of how the sword went in.

Antonio's first bull was good, fair-sized though not really big, and with adequate horns. Antonio was beautiful with the cape, moving in on the bull, taking command of him and then passing him with the wonderful, slow style. He was equally good with the muleta and killed perfectly. There were handkerchiefs all over the ring but the President would not give the ear. That they wanted something supernatural was the only explanation I could give Mary.

His second bull was not a half-bull. It looked like a three-year-old at best; was small, underweight and badly armed. The public protested it with a roar and as the Presidency allowed it to charge the picadors the protest grew. I was angry too and wondered what Antonio's managers thought they could get away with if they had chosen these bulls. It was a bull that should never have been passed by the veterinaries and never put into a formal corrida.

Antonio sent word to the President that he wanted permission to kill this bull and to pay for the substitute bull and fight and kill it at the end of the corrida. This granted he took the bull over with the muleta, passed him a couple of times to put him in place, lined him up and killed him well with a single trip in.

The bull Antonio had bought to make up for the miserable fifth animal came out of the dark of the toril carrying the biggest, widest, longest and sharpest pair of horns I had seen on a fighting bull since we had come back to Spain in 1953. He was big without being fat and he chased one of the banderilleros over the barrera and then looked for him along the top of the fence with his right horn. Antonio moved in and cited him and when the bull charged he moved the cape slowly and gently ahead of him, turning him when he wanted to, controlling him completely and giving a course in how to pass a real bull with huge horns closer and slower and more beautifully than anyone else could pass a half-bull that had been tampered with. He asked the President for only one pic so that no accident or harm would come to this bull and he told the banderilleros how he wanted the sticks placed and in what terrain.

I watched him waiting impatiently, his eyes never leaving the bull, while he noticed, analyzed, thought and planned. He told Juan where he wanted the bull placed and then he went out and took command of the bull with four low passes; his left knee, foreleg and ankle on the sand, his right leg exposed as he wove the bull back and forth with the magic of his muleta, promising him everything, offering him a target, and suavely and gently showing him that this part of the game of death did not hurt nor punish.

After these passes the bull was his and he resumed the course of showing the public what a great artist who was brave and knew bulls could do with a real bull with sturdy, long and deadly horns. He showed them all the classic passes with no tricks nor fakes nor any compromises, passing the bull as close as Jaime had but with control at all times. When he had shown them everything and how close and purely and slowly it could be done he finished off with a final pase de pecho and then lined the bull up, said good-bye to him with a final lift of the muleta, lowered it and furled it, sighted high along the sword and went in perfectly over the huge horns and the bull came out dead from under his hand while the crowd went mad. The President gave both ears while the crowd from the sun section swarmed over the fence to

carry Antonio and Jaime around the ring on their shoulders. Antonio resisted but they finally hoisted him up
and you could see this demonstration had not been set up
in advance. There were too many people and they were
too wild.

That night we slept at the Marquis del Merito's place
in the hills outside of Córdoba. It was the former Real
Monasterio de San Jeronimo de Valparaiso and is one of
the showplaces of Spain. It was wonderful climbing up
to it; up the classical bad road that leads to all great places
in Spain and seeing its Middle Ages austerity in the dark
and then waking up in the converted monastic cell of a
room to look out over the Plain of Córdoba and then
explore the gardens, the chapels and the historic rooms
in the daylight.

No one was home. Peps Merito had insisted we stay
there as the hotels are reserved far in advance and had
telephoned the caretaker from Madrid to look after us.
We had only planned to sleep there that night but Mary
had fever in the night and in the morning was too ill to
travel. We sent for a doctor from town and did not get
away until the following noon. Peps kept telephoning
from Madrid to see that everything was all right and that
we were comfortable and happy. It was a wonderful
place to stay and without the establishment it was like
camping out in a palace; a thing you rarely can do in civil
life.

We got away for Sevilla in squally weather a little after
noon next day and signed in at the old Hotel Alfonso
XIII with its comfortless grandeur and went to the Casa
Luis to eat on the way to the bullfight. It was a good meal
and a very bad bullfight.

The bulls were poor quality, uncertain in charging

and they were murdered by the pics. It was not the way the picadors used their pics or varas. They did nothing illegal in the way they pic-ed the bulls. They placed them well and solidly in the proper place, and held off the bull's charge without twisting the shafts. But there was something wrong somehow with the construction of the pics, so that the whole metal head of the shaft went into the bulls and the wooden shaft after it. The circle of metal that is supposed to keep the point from penetrating more than four and three-eighths inches disappeared into the bull with the shaft following it. The bulls were receiving media-estocadas or half-length sword wounds from the picadors and no one knew what a matador could do with his bull because it could come to him half dead and bled out. The pics are inspected and sealed by the authorities and delivered to the picador by a government functionary so you could not blame the picadors or the matadors under whose orders they work. But I had not seen pics behave like this since the bad old days in France when, if the promoters had bought six huge bulls with long, heavy horns, the arresting circle of steel on the end of the vara would sometimes and somehow turn out to be made of rubber painted with aluminum paint. These arresting circles, or redondels, could no more keep the whole head and shaft from going into the bull than a rubber dagger could penetrate flesh, and the bulls would come into the hands of the matadors half stabbed to death by the picadors. Some of us made a steady campaign against this and other abuses of the pic in the south of France in the old days and I was thoroughly familiar with all the tricks.

On this day in Sevilla as I was not down in the runway, nor in the patio de caballos before the fight, since I was looking after Mary who no longer had fever but was still ill and tired, I had no chance to examine the pics. They had been inspected and passed so they had to be okay. But they did horrible damage to the bulls.

After the fight Antonio said the pic on his second bull had hit a vein. This was very true. It had gone in deep enough to hit several and if the picador had not gotten it out finally it would have hit a big artery. As it was the blood was bright, pumping from the jagged wound down the bull's shoulder and down his leg and trailed in clotted strings on the sand.

I knew how great Antonio could be with any bulls for which there was a way of fighting. At Christmas I had written him that I wanted to come over and write the truth, the absolute truth, about his work and his place in bullfighting so there would be a permanent record; something that would last when we were both gone. He wanted me to do this and he knew he could handle anything that came out of the toril. Now for two days small and immature bulls had come out for him and that was somebody's fault. He had been disgusted each time and the big-horned bull in Córdoba had cost him forty thousand pesetas. Nobody was happy at the end of that bullfight in Sevilla.

Bill and I got off at first light in the morning to drive back to Madrid. The girls were going to sleep late and then drive the small gray Volkswagen to Málaga on the beautiful road through Antequera and then come up to meet us at Granada where Luis Miguel would be fighting on one day and Antonio on another. Mary had no fever when she had gone to sleep and I hoped a day's rest and the sun at the Consula would put her in shape. The schedule was brutal though but after Granada the next fights we planned to go to were all within easy range of Málaga where we were based.

Driving to Madrid through low, driving clouds and rain we could not see the country except in breaks in the weather. We were both sad as the weather about the fights, the underweight and immature bulls that some-one had tried to slip in and Bill was pessimistic about the season. Neither of us cared truly for Sevilla. This is heresy in Andalucia and in bullfighting. People who care about bullfighting are supposed to have a mystic feeling about Sevilla. But I had come to believe over many years that there are more bad bullfights there in proportion to those given than in any other city.

We saw some big flights of storks searching daintily for food in the rain and many different kinds of hawks in the wild country. Hawks always make me happy and they were all out in the wild weather having a hard time making a living as the wind held the ground birds so close to cover. From Bailén on, the road we were to get to know so well untaped itself toward the central plateau and in the breaks in the weather the castles and the small white villages unsheltered from the wind—there was no way to shelter them because there were so many winds as you moved north—stood rain-washed in the storm-flattened fields of grain and the vines that seemed to have grown a half a hand higher since we had passed south three days before.

We stopped for gas and had a glass of wine or slice of cheese or a few olives in the bar of the filling station and drank black coffee. Bill never drank wine when he was driving but I kept a cold bottle of the light *rosado* of Campanas in the ice bag and ate bread with a slab of Manchegan cheese with it. I loved this country in all seasons and was always happy to come through the last pass and move into the harshness of La Mancha and Castille.

Bill did not want to eat until we should reach Madrid.

He believed food made him sleepy on the road and he was starting to train for the all-day and all-night drives we knew that we would have. He loved food and knew good food and where to get it in any country better than anyone I had ever known. When he came to Spain first he had based in Madrid and then had driven with Annie through every province in Spain. There was no town in Spain he did not know, and he knew the wines, the local cooking, the special things to eat and the good places to eat in all the towns large and small. He was a wonderful travelling companion for me and he was an iron man driving.

We got into Madrid in time for a late lunch at the Callejón, a narrow, crowded restaurant on the Calle Becerra where we always ate when we were alone because we both thought that, day in and day out, it had the best food in town. It had a different regional specialty each day but it always had the best vegetables, fish, meats and fruits that were in the markets and simple, wonderful cooking. There was tinto, clarete and Valdepeñas wine in small, medium or big pitchers and the wine was excellent.

Bill deployed his appetite after we had drunk a few glasses of Valdepeñas drawn from the barrel at the tavern bar in the entry where we waited for a table. There was a notation on the menu that one order of anything would fill you and he ordered a grilled sole followed by a regional specialty from Asturias that would do exactly what the menu said for at least two people. He downed this and said, "The food is quite good here."

After the second large pitcher of Valdepeñas he said, "So is the wine."

I was eating a delicate order of fried baby eels in garlic that resembled bamboo sprouts slightly crisped at the tips but had a more lubricious texture. They filled a large

deep dish and were heavenly to eat and hell on anyone you met afterwards in a closed room or even in the open air.

"Eels are excellent," I said. "Can't really tell about the wine yet. Care for any eels?"

"Perhaps a single order," Bill said. "Try the wine. You may like it."

"Another large pitcher please," I said to the waiter.

"Yes, Don Ernesto. Here it is. I had it waiting."

The proprietor came over.

"What about a steak?" he asked. "We have very good ones today."

"Save it for this evening. What about some asparagus?"

"Very good," he said. "From Aranjuez."

"We have bulls in Aranjuez tomorrow," I said.

"How is Antonio?"

"Fine. He drove up last night from Sevilla. We drove up this morning."

"How was Sevilla?"

"So-so. Bulls worthless."

"Will you and he eat here tonight?"

"I don't think so."

"I'll keep the private room if you want it. Did they enjoy the last meal?"

"Very much."

"Good luck in Aranjuez."

"Thank you," I said.

We had very bad luck in Aranjuez but I felt no presentiments or forebodings.

The day before while Antonio was fighting in Sevilla Luis Miguel was fighting in Toledo with Antonio Bienvenida and Jaime Ostos. The ring was sold out. It was a miserable, rainy day and the bulls were good-sized and uneven in their bravery. The horns, according to all reports I heard, were badly cut down. Luis Miguel was good with his first bull and very good with his second bull. He cut the ear of the second bull after working him beautifully and would have had both ears if he had been luckier with the sword.

I was very sorry not to have seen Luis Miguel fight especially as we would miss him the next day at Granada. But that was the way the dates were going now and I knew we would catch up with him soon. I had a list of his firm engagements and of Antonio's and shortly they would be fighting in the same ferias and the same towns. Then they would be fighting on the same programs and then I knew they would have to fight alone together. Meantime I kept track of Miguel as well as I could through people I trusted who were seeing his fights.

ERNEST HEMINGWAY

CHAPTER

5

IT WAS A GOOD DAY FOR BULLS AT ARANJUEZ ON MAY THIRTI-eth. The rain was gone and the town was new-washed in the sun. The trees were green and the cobbled streets were not yet dusty. There were many country people in black smocks and the iron-hard striped gray trousers of the province and a good crowd from Madrid. We went to the old café-restaurant under the shade of trees and watched the river and the excursion boats. The river was brown and swollen from the rains.

Afterwards our two guests went to see the royal gardens up the river and Bill and I walked over the bridge and to the old Hotel Delicias to see Antonio and pick up the paper from Miguelillo, his sword handler. I paid Miguelillo for the four barrera seats, warned a young Spanish reporter who was writing a series of articles on Antonio for a Madrid paper not to bother him at this time but let him rest, and explained why, and went over to the bed to speak to Antonio and set an example to the followers by leaving quickly.

"Will you drive straight through to Granada or stop on the way to sleep?" he asked.

"I thought we'd sleep at Manzanares."

"Bailén is better," he said. "I'll drive the car for you and we can talk and then eat at Bailén. Then I'll go on to Granada in the Mercedes and sleep on the way."

"Where will we meet?"

"Here after the fight."

"Good," I said. "Until then."

He smiled and I could see he felt good and very solid. I got the young reporter from *El Pueblo* out of the room with us. Miguelillo was setting up the portable religious equipment. The heavy embossed leather sword case leaned against the wall beside the dressing table where he was setting out the scapularies and the oil lamp to burn before the picture of the Virgin.

The mud around the small, old, beautiful, uncomfortable, decaying ring was drying and the dust was forming. We went in and found our places and looked down on the immediate intimacy of the sand.

Antonio had the first Sánchez Cobaleda bull. He was big, black and handsome with big horns with very sharp points. Antonio took him with the cape with the slow, confident, low, sweeping elegance of his veronicas, moving in on him as far as he could go and then controlling his charges to pass him slower and slower and as close as the horns could come by. The crowd did not light up as it would have in Madrid so he made the next quite with chicuelinas less dangerous, less classical but a delicate piece of Sevillian embroidery with the cape. He offered the cape to the bull, holding it at the height of his chest. Then he turned slowly with the cape wrapping itself around him spinning slowly into and out of trouble at each charge of the bull. It is very pretty to watch but basically it is a trick, not a pass. The bull starts to pass but the man spins slowly away from him as the bull comes into his territory. The crowd liked this. We liked it too. It is always pretty but it does not do anything to you inside.

Antonio's bull came to the muleta more than a little dangerous on both the right and the left and he worked him low as he had worked the bull in Córdoba to straighten him out and give him confidence. Something had happened in the bull's head; perhaps the chicuelinas had disillusioned him. I have seen that happen. Now Antonio had to take him from very close to start him. It was not a question of a change in his vision. It was something that was going on in that ten minutes of education the bull receives that teaches him how to die.

Antonio gave him confidence by letting him have the right leg and thigh as a solid planted objective and then showing him how he could follow the lure without pain and that it could be a game.

Then they played the game together with either hand, round and round. High up and down stairs. Take it now, bull. Wrap around me nice, bull. Try it again, bull. Once more.

Then the bull had one small thought when Antonio was winding him around him. He broke off the game in the middle of a long pass and saw the body and tried for it. The horn missed by a hundredth of an inch and the bull's head bumped Antonio as he passed. Antonio looked back at him, picked him up with the muleta and passed him close by his chest.

Then he repeated the whole lesson to the bull, and made him do the exact pass where he had nearly caught him twice more. The crowd was with him completely now and he was working to the music they had called for. Finally he killed. He went in well and the sword hit a bare touch off center. The whole ring asked for the ear

and waved their handkerchiefs. But the bull had gone
down bleeding from the mouth as many properly killed
bulls will and the President refused the ear although the
crowd kept up their waving until the bull was dragged
out.

Antonio had to circle the ring and come out twice to
salute the crowd. He came in cold and angry and detached and said something to Miguelillo when he gave
him a glass of water. He drank a little looking out at
nothing and then rinsed his mouth and spat the water
out onto the sand. Later I asked Miguelillo what he had
said.

"What do I have to do to cut an ear, he told me. Well,
he showed them."

Chicuelo II was the second matador. He is, or was,
small, not over five feet two inches, grave, with a dig-
nified, sad face. He is braver than a badger or than any
animal and most men I think and he came to bullfighting
as a novillero and then matador in 1953 and 1954 from
the terrible school of the capeas. These are informal
bullfights in village squares in Castille and La Mancha
and to a lesser extent in other provinces where the local
boys and travelling troupes of aspirant toreros fight bulls
that have sometimes been fought again and again. Animals have been fought in capeas that have previously
killed more than ten men. They are fought in towns and
villages that cannot afford a bull ring and carts are piled
around to block the exits from the square and long, stout,
sharp-pointed shepherd's or herdsmen's rods are hawked
to the spectators so that they may poke the amateur
bullfighters back into the ring or beat them if they try
to escape.

Chicuelo II was a star of the capeas until he was
twenty-five years old. All the time the name bullfighters
in the time of Manolete and after were facing bulls and

half-bulls and three-year-olds with their horns cut down he had been fighting bulls up to seven years old with intact horns. Many of these bulls had been fought previously and so were as dangerous as any wild animal that lives. He had been fighting in villages where there were no infirmaries nor hospitals nor surgeons. To survive he had to know about bulls and how to keep close to them without being caught. He knew how to stay alive with bulls that were odds on each time to kill him and he had learned to do every tricky pass there was to do and every circus trick. He also learned how to kill bulls competently and well and he had a skillful and marvellous left hand that protected him as he went in to kill and lowered the bull's head perfectly to compensate for his short stature. Also he was, besides being absolutely brave, supremely lucky.

This season he had come out of retirement because he was bored doing anything but fighting bulls. He had retired because he knew he was lucky and that you could only let the bet ride so many times. He had come back because nothing else was really any fun. There was, also, as always, the money.

He drew a good bull big enough in contrast to his own diminutive stature to make the animal look huge. The bull had two good horns and Chicuelo II gave his justly celebrated course of how to stay alive in the bull ring and spend the time closer to the bull than anyone else could go with sanity. He went with sanity, marvellous reflexes and his wonderful luck and he made a number of good passes and every tricky pass and every circus pass in the book and did them well. It would be much more dangerous to take the bull from further away and pass him classically. But it didn't look that way and Chicuelo did everything backwards that he could, looking out at the crowd as the bull moved under his extended arm to

remind them of Manolete who, with his manager, had
brought bullfighting to its second lowest ebb and then
been killed and dying had become a demi-god and so
escaped criticism forever.

The crowd loved Chicuelo II and rightly. He was one
of them and he gave them what they had been taught to
believe was bullfighting and he was doing it with a real
bull. He needed luck to do it but he also needed great
knowledge and the purest of courage. He hit bone once
when he went in to kill and then went in and buried the
sword in high up, cradling himself in the horns as his
fine left hand brought the bull out dead under the flat of
his hand.

The President gave him both ears and he circled the
ring with them; gravely pleased. I like to think of him as
he was all that summer and it is no good to think of what
happened when his luck ran out.

Antonio's second bull came out handsome, shining
black, well-horned and brave. He came in beautifully
and I saw Antonio wanted to take him immediately. He
had started out with the cape when an aspirant
bullfighter, a fairly competent, good-looking kid in cap,
light shirt and blue trousers jumped out of the sun section on our left, vaulted the fence and spread his muleta
out in front of the bull. While Ferrer, Joni and Juan,
Antonio's three banderilleros, raced for him to catch him
and turn him over to the police before the bull should
gore him and be ruined for the fight, the boy made three
or four good passes. He took advantage of the bull's
natural brío and put himself athwart his charges having,
at the same time, to avoid three fast men trying to catch
him and put him out of the ring.

Nothing can spoil a bull for a matador so rapidly and
completely as the intrusion of an espontáneo in the fight.
The bull learns with every pass and a great bullfighter

does not make a single pass without intending to lead toward a definite result. If the bull catches a man and gores him at the start of the fight, he will have lost all innocence of previous contact with a man on foot that the formal corrida is based on. But I watched Antonio watching the boy making his passes skillfully and well and in spite of the fact that the boy was exposing Antonio to disaster I saw he was not worried. He was studying the bull and learning with each move he made.

Joni and Ferrer caught the boy finally and he went quietly to the barrera. Antonio ran over to him with the cape, said something to him very quickly and put his arm around him and hugged him. Then he went out with the cape and took the bull over. He knew him now and he had sized him up completely.

His first passes were the uncopiable, slow-measured elegance that seemed endless as he moved the cape ahead of the bull. The public knew that they were seeing something now that they had never seen and that there was no trick. They had never seen a matador congratulate and forgive someone who could have ruined his bull for him and now they were appreciating something that, before, on the first bull, they had seen but not appreciated. Antonio was using the cape as no one alive had ever used it.

He led the bull over to one of the Salas brothers for him to pic and said, "Be careful of him and do what I say."

The bull was brave and strong and pushed hard under the steel which was placed perfectly. Antonio took him away and made the same slow, beautiful veronicas again.

On the second charge with the pic well placed the bull knocked the horse over and threw Salas against the planks of the barrera.

Juan, his brother and confidential banderillero,

wanted the bull to charge the horses again as he was very strong and could have taken two more pics to tire his neck muscles and bring his head down so he would be easier to kill.

"Don't give me lessons," Antonio told him. "I want him the way he is."

Antonio signalled to the President, asking him for permission to change to the banderillas. After a single pair of banderillas he asked permission again to take the bull with the muleta.

He took the bull with the muleta so suavely, so simply, and so smoothly that every pass seemed to be sculptured. He made all the classic passes and then seemed to try to refine them and make them purer in line and more dangerous as he purposely shortened his naturales by bringing his elbow in to bring the bull by him closer than it seemed any bull could be passed. It was a big bull, entire, brave and strong and with good horns and Antonio made the most complete and classic faena with him that I had ever seen.

Then with it all done and the bull ready to kill I thought he was going crazy. He began to make the trick passes of Manolete that Chicuelo II had used just to show the public if that was what they wanted here was how it should be done. He was working the bull in the sand of the ring where the last three bulls had been pic-ed and the sand was torn up and furrowed by the hooves. As he took the bull from behind him to pass him in a pass that is called the girardilla, the bull's right hind hoof slipped and he lurched and his right horn drove into Antonio's left buttock. There is no less-romantic nor more dangerous place to be gored and he had bought this wound himself and he knew it, knew how grave it was and hated it and the chance that he might be prevented from killing the bull and wiping out his mistake. The bull hit him solidly. I saw the horn go in and lift Antonio off the ground. But he landed on his feet and did not fall.

The blood was coming fast now and he leaned with his rump against the red planks of the barrera as though to staunch the flow. I was watching Antonio and I did not see who had taken the bull away. Little Miguelillo had been the first one over the barrera and he held Antonio up by one arm as Domingo Dominguín, his manager, and Pepé his brother vaulted into the ring. Everyone saw the gravity of the horn wound and his brother, his manager and his sword handler grabbed him and tried to hold him and make him go to the infirmary. Antonio shook them all off in a rage saying to Pepé, "And you call yourself an Ordóñez."

He went out to the bull bleeding heavily and raging. I had seen him terribly angry in the ring before and he fought often in a mixture of beatitude and intelligent, deadly anger. But he was going to kill this bull as well as a bull could be killed and he knew he had to kill him very promptly or bleed out and faint.

He lined the bull up and I watched him drop the muleta low, low, low, and sighting for the death hole in the top between the shoulder blades, go in perfectly and come out over the horn. Then he raised his hand as he faced the bull and commanded him to go down with the death that he had placed inside him.

He stood there and bled and would not let anyone touch him until the bull staggered and rolled over. He stood there bleeding and his people were afraid to touch him after they heard what he said to them until the President, answering the waving handkerchiefs and the shouting, signalled for both the ears and the tail and a foot to be cut. He waited until the trophies were brought and I watched him standing there bleeding as I made my way through the crowd toward the ring entrance that would lead to the infirmary. Then he turned and took two steps to start circling the ring, and then slid into the arms of Ferrer and Domingo. He was perfectly conscious but he knew he was bleeding out and there was nothing any more that he could do. That afternoon was over and he had to get ready to return to fight.

In the infirmary Dr. Tamames went into the wound, saw what he had to deal with and how grave it was, did the immediately necessary, closed the wound and rushed Antonio to the hospital Ruber in Madrid for operation. Outside the door of the infirmary the boy who had jumped into the ring was crying.

Antonio was just coming out from the anaesthetic when we reached the Ruber clinic. The wound was six inches deep in the gluteal muscle of the left leg. The horn had gone in just beside the rectum, almost touching it, and had ripped through the muscles up to the sciatic nerve. Dr. Tamames told me that an eighth of an inch to the right it would have penetrated the rectum and gone into the intestine. Less than an eighth deeper it would have hit the sciatic nerve. Tamames had opened it, cleaned it, repaired the damage and sewed up the wound leaving a drain which worked on suction with a clockwork device. You could hear it tick like a metronome.

Antonio had heard it before. This was his twelfth grave horn wound. His face was serious but he smiled with his eyes.

"Ernesto," he said, pronouncing it "Airnesthto," in Andaluz.

"Do you hurt bad?"

"Not yet," he said. "Later."

"Don't talk," I said. "Rest as easy as you can. Manolo says it's okay. If you had to take one you couldn't have taken it in a better place. I'll tell you anything he tells me. I'll go now. Take it as easy as you can."

"When will you be back?"

"Tomorrow when you wake up."

Carmen had been sitting by the bed holding his hand. She kissed him and he closed his eyes. He was not really awake yet and the real pain had not started.

Carmen came outside the hospital room with me and I told her what Tamames had told me. Her father was a matador. She had three brothers who were matadors and now she was married to a matador. She was beautiful, lovely and loving and calm in all emergency and disaster. She had been through the awful part now and her job was just beginning. She had had the job once a year each year since she had married Antonio.

"How did it really happen?" she asked me.

"There was no reason for it to happen. It never had to happen. He doesn't have to fight backwards."

"You tell him."

"He knows it. I don't have to tell him."

"You tell him anyway, Ernesto."

"He doesn't have to compete with Chicuelo II," I said. "He's competing with history."

"I know," she said; and I knew that she was thinking that soon her husband would be competing with her favorite brother and history would be looking on. I remembered how three years before we had been talking at dinner in their flat and someone had said how wonderful it would be and how much money they would make if Luis Miguel would come back to the ring and fight mano a mano with Antonio.

"Don't talk about it," she had said. "They'd kill each other."

This night she said, "Good-bye, Ernesto. I hope he can sleep."

Bill Davis and I stayed in Madrid until Antonio was

out of danger. After the first night the pain really started and it increased up to and past the limit of tolerance. The clockwork suction pump kept the wound drawing but it was swollen and taut under the dressing. I hated to watch Antonio suffer and I did not want to be a witness to the agony he went through and how he fought not to let the pain humiliate him as it rose in force like a wind ascending the Beaufort scale. I would say it was at about Force Ten, or just past Full Gale as we measure pain in our family, on the day we were waiting for Tamames to come to remove the first dressing. This is the time when you know, except for possible complications, whether you have won or not. If there is no gangrene and the wound is clean you have won and with a wound like this your man can fight again in three weeks or under depending on morale and training.

"Where is he?" Antonio asked. "He was going to be here at eleven."

"He's on another floor," I said.

"If they could quiet the ticking machine," he said. "I can stand everything but the ticking."

Wounded matadors who are going to fight again as soon as possible are given a minimum of sedation. The theory is that they must have nothing that will affect their nerves or their reflexes. In an American hospital they might have kept him out of pain, "snowed" it is called. In Spain pain is quite simply regarded as something a man has to take. Whether the pain is not as bad for a man's nerves as the drug that would stop it is not considered.

"Can't you give him something to ease him?" I had asked Manolo Tamames earlier.

"I gave him something last night," Tamames said. "He's a matador, Ernesto."

He was a matador all right and Manolo Tamames was

a great surgeon and a true friend but it is a rough theory when you watch it practiced.

Antonio wanted me to stay with him.

"Is it any better at all?"

"It's bad, Ernesto, bad, bad. Maybe he can shift the tube when he opens it up. Where do you think he is?"

"I'll send and find out."

It was a bright cool day outside with a breeze off the Guadarramas and it was cool and pleasant in the darkened room but Antonio was sweating heavily with the pain and he held his gray lips together. He did not want to open his lips but his eyes kept asking for Tamames to come. The outer room was full of people all sitting silently or whispering. Miguelillo was taking telephone calls. Antonio's mother, a dark-faced, handsome woman, buxom, her hair pulled straight back, was in or out of the room, sitting in a corner and fanning herself or coming to sit by the bed. Carmen was taking telephone calls in another room when she was not sitting by the bed. Outside in the hall the picadors and banderilleros sat or stood. Visitors came and went leaving messages and cards. Miguelillo kept everyone but the family out of the room.

Finally Tamames came in, followed by two nurses, and cleared everyone out that shouldn't see what was going to happen. He was brusque and gray and joking as always.

"What's the matter with you?" he said to Antonio. "Do you think I don't have other patients?"

"Come here," he said to me. "Distinguished colleague. Stand here. Roll him over. Roll over yourself, you, and lie on your face. You're in no danger from Ernesto or me."

He cut away the big dressing and when he lifted the gauze packing he smelled it quickly and handed it to me.

I smelled it and dropped it in the basin the nurse held. There was no odor of gangrene. Tamames looked at me and grinned. The wound was clean. It was a little angry-looking around four of the long line of stitches but it looked good. Tamames snipped the rubber tube of the drain, leaving just a short length.

"No more tic-toc," he said. "Calm your little nerves."

He cleaned, sifted and dressed rapidly and then had me help tape the dressing on.

"Now your pain. Your famous pain," he said. "The dressing had to be fastened on securely. You understand? The wound swells. That is natural. You can't poke something bigger around than a hoe handle six inches up into you there and make all that destruction in the muscle without making a wound that will pain and swell. The dressing constricts it and that makes it worse. Now this dressing is comfortable. Isn't it?"

"Yes," said Antonio.

"Then let's have no more about pain."

"You didn't feel the big pain," I said.

"Neither did you," Tamames said. "Fortunately."

We went over in the corner and the family came back to the bedside.

"How long Manolo?" I asked.

"He'll fight in three weeks if there are no complications. It's a very big wound Ernesto and there was much destruction. I'm sorry he had so much pain."

"He had plenty."

"Will he come to you at Málaga to get in shape?"

"Yes."

"Good. I'll ship him down as soon as he can travel."

"I'll leave tomorrow night if he is okay and has no fever. I have a lot of work to do."

"Good. I'll tell you if he is okay to leave."

I left word we would be back in the evening. There

was much family and old friends now and I wanted to get out with Bill into the daylight and the town. We knew it would be all right now and I did not want to intrude. There was still time to get to the Prado while the light was good. They have vintage lights there at different hours of the day.

When Antonio and Carmen came off the plane at the cheerful little Málaga airport he was leaning heavily on a cane and I had to help him out through the waiting room and into the car. It was a week since I had left him at the hospital. He and Carmen were both dead tired from the trip and we all had a quiet supper and I helped get him to their bedroom.

"You wake up early don't you, Ernesto?" he said. I knew he usually slept until noon when he was travelling and fighting and sometimes later.

"Sure, but you sleep late. Sleep as late as you can and rest."

"I want to get out with you. I'm always up early on the ranch."

In the early morning before the dew had dried in the gardens he had made his way up the stairs and down the hall with the cane to my room.

"Do you want to walk?" he asked.

"Sure."

"Let's go," he said. He laid the cane down on my bed. "The cane's finished," he said. "You keep the cane."

We walked for about a half an hour, me holding him carefully by the arm so he would not fall.

"What a garden," he said. "It's bigger than the Botánico in Madrid."

"The house is a little smaller than the Escorial. But on the other hand there are no kings buried in it and you can drink wine and it is permitted to sing."

In nearly all Spanish bars and bodegas there is a sign that it is not permitted to sing.

"We'll sing," he said. We walked as long as I thought he could stand it. Then he said, "I have a letter for you from Tamames giving all the treatment to follow."

I hoped we had the necessary medicines and vitamins, or that I would be able to get them in Málaga or find them in Gibraltar.

"Let's go to the house and I'll get it so we can start. We don't want to lose any time."

I left him in the hallway and he made his way, trying to walk steadily but touching the wall with one hand, to their room. He came back with a small visiting card envelope addressed to me. I opened it and took out the card and read, "Distinguished colleague: I hereby deliver over to your care my client Antonio Ordóñez. If you have to operate: *con mano duro* [use a strong and steady hand]. Signed Manolo Tamames."

"Ernesto, should we start the treatment?"

"I think we might have a single glass of Campanas rosado," I said.

"Do you think that's indicated?" Antonio asked.

"Not usually this early in the morning, but as a mild laxative."

"Can we swim?"

"Not until it warms up at noon."

"Maybe the cold water would be good for it."

"Maybe you'd get a sore throat too."

"My sore throat is over. Let's swim now."

"We'll swim when the sun warms up the water."

"All right. Let's walk some more. Tell me about everything that's happened. Did you write well?"

"Some days very well. Some days not so good."

"I'm the same way. There are days when you can't

Luis Miguel Domingín in 1954, training for his return to the ring. Photo by A. E. Hotchner.

Hemingway with Dominguín and his friend Ava Gardner,
1954. Photo by A. E. Hotchner.

Antonio Ordóñez watching Dominguín at work during one of their mano a mano bullfights. Photo © Larry Burrows.

Antonio Ordóñez performing a pase de pecho, Bilbao, 1952. Photo by Cuevas, courtesy the John F. Kennedy Library.

Dominguín citing for banderillas and placing them, Valencia, 1959. He was acknowledged a master of this phase of the bullfight. Photos by Cuevas, courtesy the John F. Kennedy Library.

Dominguín performing two of the "tricks" that Hemingway disliked: kissing the bull and pretending to call it on the telephone. Photos by Cuevas, courtesy the John F. Kennedy Library.

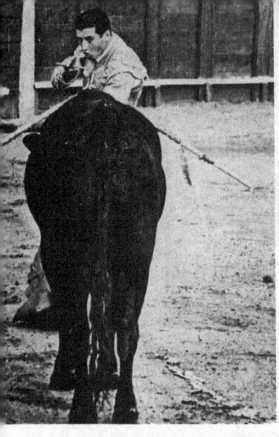

Ordóñez citing for the kill, Logroño, 1955. Photo by Cuevas, courtesy the John F. Kennedy Library.

Ordóñez performing a derechazo de rodillas, a right-handed pass with the muleta, performed on one knee. Photo courtesy the John F. Kennedy Library.

Ordóñez being carried from the ring after being gored at Aran-juez on May 30, 1959. He still holds the bull's tail, which was awarded him along with both ears and the hoof. Photo by Cuevas, courtesy the John F. Kennedy Library.

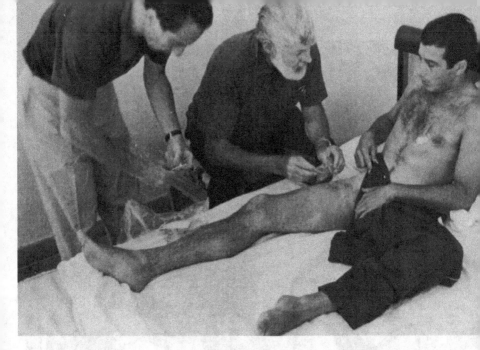

Hemingway and A. E. Hotchner tending Ordóñez's cornada. Photo © Larry Burrows.

Hemingway and Ordóñez shooting skeet at La Consula, Bill Davis's home near Málaga, where Ordóñez came to convalesce after being gored. A. E. Hotchner assisting. Photo © Larry Burrows.

write at all. But they have paid to see you so you write as well as you can."

"You've been writing all right lately."

"Yes. But you know what I mean. You have days too when it isn't there."

"Yes. But I always force it and I use my head."

"So do I. But it's wonderful when you really write. There's nothing better."

He was very pleased, always, to call the faena writing.

We talked about all sorts of things: the different problems of the artist in the world he lives in; technical things and professional secrets; finance; sometimes economics and politics. Sometimes women, very often women and how we should try to be good husbands, then perhaps women, other people's women, and our daily lives and problems. We talked all summer and all fall driving after fights to other fights and at meals and at strange hours during the recuperation times. We practiced for fun and as a game judging people the minute you saw them as you would bulls. But that was later.

That first day at La Consula we talked and joked, happy to have the wound over and the rebuilding started. Antonio swam a little the first day. The wound was still drawing and I changed the small dressing. The second day he walked carefully but with no limp nor unsteadiness. Each day he was stronger and better. We exercised, swam, shot hand trap in the olive orchard behind the stables and trained well and ate and drank well and had fun. Then he overreached and went down to bathe in the sea on a rough day and the tumbling sand-filled breakers opened the wound partially but I could see it was healing soundly and well and I cleaned it and dressed it and taped it together.

Everybody was happy and it was as though Carmen

and Antonio were on their honeymoon. The necessity to convalesce after the goring had given them a chance for a short time of normal married life in the month of June and while it was dearly paid for in blood and loss of earnings they were both making the most of it and Carmen was more beautiful each day.

They left finally for the ranch they owned, and were still paying for, at Valcargado in the rolling hills in the Medina Sidonia country below Cádiz. I put a last dressing on the wound for the trip in the Chevrolet medium truck chassis that had been converted into a travelling bus for the cuadrilla with their equipment. We all said good-bye and they were off through the gate with Antonio driving.

6

Luis Miguel had fought four times since Antonio had been wounded at Aranjuez and all the reports had said that he was terrific. I had seen Miguel and talked with him when he had come up from his great successes in Granada to visit Antonio in the hospital and I was very anxious to see him fight. I had promised him that we would see him in Algeciras where he was to fight twice.

It was a beautiful trip along the coast road to Algeciras on a bright windy day. I was worried about the effect of the wind on the fight but the Algeciras ring is placed and built so that it gives fine protection from the heavy east wind they call the Levante. This wind is the curse of coastal Andalucia as the Mistral is of Provence but it did not bother the bullfighters although the flag on the staff at the top of the ring was whipping stiffly.

Luis Miguel was as good as all the reports of him had been. He was proud without being arrogant, tranquil, at ease in the ring at all times and in full control of everything that went on. It was a pleasure to see him direct the fight and to watch his intelligence at work. He had the complete and respectful concentration on his work which marks all great artists.

With the cape he was better than I remembered him but his veronicas did not move me. But the varied repertoire of his passes was delightful. They were infinitely skillful and perfectly executed.

He was a masterful banderillero and he put in three pairs that were equal to the work of the finest banderilleros I had seen. They were not circus nor on a basis of posturing. He did not gallop in on the bull but caught his attention from the start and brought him to the contact, leading him in by an exercise in geometry until, as the horn reached for the man, he raised his arms high and dropped the sticks into the exact spot where they should go.

His work with the muleta was effective and interesting. His classic passes were well made and he had a great variety of all types of passes and used them extensively. He killed skillfully without exposing himself excessively. I could see he could kill really well if he wanted to. I could also see why he had been the number one bullfighter in Spain and the world (that is the Spanish way of ranking the places) for many years. I could see what dangerous competition he would be for Antonio and watching Luis Miguel in both of his bulls—he was even better in the second—I had not one doubt in my mind as to how the competition would come out. I was sure after I watched Luis Miguel do his trick with the bull when, after preparing him with the muleta, he tossed the muleta and the sword aside and knelt carefully inside the bull's angle of vision unarmed in front of the bull's horns.

The crowd loved this but when I had seen it twice I knew how it was done. I had seen something else too.

The horns of Luis Miguel's bulls had been cut off at the points, then shaved back to normal shape and I could see the shine of the used crankcase oil that hid the manipulations that had been made and gave them the healthy-looking polish of normal horns. The horns looked fine unless you knew how to look at horns.

Luis Miguel was in wonderful shape, he was a great bullfighter, he had enormous class, great knowledge, great charm in the ring as well as out of it, and he was a very dangerous competitor. He looked just a little too finely drawn for this early in the season with an arduous schedule ahead. I knew, though, that Antonio had one definite advantage at this stage of the duel. He had been fighting bulls with horns that had not been tampered with in Madrid and I had seen him with the huge horned bull at Córdoba. I was watching Miguel with bulls whose horns had been fixed.

Knowledgeable people who sat near us knew it and they did not care. They came for the spectacle. Others were in the business and they did not care. It was part of the business. Most of the people did not know it. I knew it and I cared because I believed, watching him, that Miguel had a great sense and knowledge of bulls and he could have fought any kind of bulls and ranked with the truly great; maybe with Joselito. But a diet of this type of bull with his defenses altered would unfit him, subtly but permanently, for the real bulls when he had to face them.

After the corrida we found Miguelillo, who was to guide us out to Antonio's ranch. We drove out of town in the dark and onto the road that climbed around and out of the wild, western buttress of Europe away from the sea and into the country of streams, drained lagoons and rolling hills that led past the magic, white, high-perched town of Vejar to the country road that went back around the hills to Antonio's ranch. We came in late, had dinner at midnight and went to bed soon after. The ranch was a nice spread of about three thousand acres with good natural feed and very good water. He had breeding cows, yearlings, two seed bulls and one corrida of six novillos and one of six full bulls ready to go. The pasture and holding grounds had never been used for fighting stock before so it was clean. Antonio had a good piece of the ranch planted in grain. It was being cut now and we went out and looked everything over in the Land-Rover in the very early morning.

Back at the white-washed ranch house with its barns, stables, chicken runs, court yards and storage buildings all more or less connecting with the living quarters we heard that Luis Miguel, Jaime Ostos and two bull breeders were coming to lunch.

It was a long, gay, heavy lunch with the four visitors, Antonio and I and Rupert sitting at a table in the sun room and our women, Bill and a Valencian couple, great friends of Carmen and Antonio, at another table in the big dark cool dining room. It reminded me somehow of those meals in the war when one of two generals who hated each other ever since West Point would be the host at his headquarters and the two generals would lunch in super friendliness watching each other hopefully for any evidence of slowing down, new defects, uneasiness or decay. It was a very hearty lunch and everyone made fun of everyone else but a little carefully and with the barbs drawn. Luis Miguel and I were a little rough with each other; but carefully rough. We were all being friends. I really was and he was too. But between him and Antonio the chips had been down for a long time. It was nice of him to have come out to Antonio's ranch for the first time and Carmen had appreciated it and it made her happy.

We left for the Consula after three days. They had been good days and I knew that Antonio had no problems in his head about the wound and that he was sleeping well and mending fast. We were to meet at Algeciras in four days where Luis Miguel was fighting again. On the Monday after the fight we would make a one-day trip to Ronda. Then he would go back to the ranch and start training with the breeding stock that was being tested and we would go on down over the mountains to La Consula and work until he started fighting.

The Pablo Romero bulls that Luis Miguel fought at Algeciras were in as good condition, as sound in their hooves and legs, and as fast as the Pablo Romeros Antonio had fought in Madrid had been overweight, loggy and crippled. Luis Miguel was superb all afternoon. He did not look as drawn as he had looked the week before but perhaps that was because he'd had a week's rest from fighting. He took the first bull with both knees on the sand and made a beautiful larga. All his cape work was excellent and his veronicas were the best I had seen him make. He dedicated the bull to Mary and to me, calling her name out loud and clear so she would know it was for her and stand up. We were a third of the way up in the stands in seats over an entrance to the barreras and, standing, could not hear what he said but could only watch his dark face and see his lips move. Mary was very excited and was blushing. Then Luis Miguel sailed the heavy hat up like a ballplayer. I caught it and handed it to Mary and we sat down to watch him do a wonderful faena with the muleta directly below us adjusting himself to the bull and to his speed, controlling him and passing him slowly and beautifully in all his long and varied repertoire with the muleta. He hit bone twice when he went in to kill and each time he went in so well

that the attempt was worth an estocada. The third time
he put the sword in all the way. The public wanted an
ear for him because of the sincerity of his two voyages
in with the sword but the President refused it. The
crowd was indignant and made him circle the ring twice.

With his second bull Luis Miguel was even better. The
bull was perfect. He did not have a defect and Miguel
saw it instantly and made six veronicas without moving
the position of his feet. He put in three pairs of banderillas poder a poder of the same type as in the last fight,
citing the bull and bringing him onto him as he moved
in until each met at full force then swinging out over the
horn as the poised sticks descended vertically in the exact
centimeter of space where they belonged. He was a wonderful banderillero and I was deeply moved and im-
pressed by his skill, his knowledge and his artistry. He
was doing everything with an easy grace and confidence
and he seemed both happy and supremely secure in all
that he did.

Then he hypnotized the bull with the slow swaying
back and forth of the spread muleta in front of his eyes
that I had spotted before. It made the bull dizzy and fixed
him temporarily. You can do the same thing with a
chicken by tucking its head under its wing and swaying
it back and forth with your hands a half dozen times. You
can lay the chicken down with its head still under its
wing and it will lie, hypnotized, for an hour or more or
until you wake it. It was a parlor trick that had much
success in East Africa. Sometimes I would have a dozen
chickens lying asleep in a row on the porch of some
native hut in a village under Kilimanjaro when we
needed something badly and it was necessary to make
magic to obtain it.

Luis Miguel hypnotized the bull with the sleep-rock-
ing passes and then knelt before him inside his field of

vision and discarded his sword and muleta and turned his back on him. This was what Antonio and I called the truco or the trick. It was a good trick but it was a trick. Luis Miguel's work had been so superior and so brilliant that he had not needed the trick. But he used it for insurance against the President and the public.

When he roused the bull and squared him for the kill he went in well with the sword and then severed the spinal marrow with the first thrust of the descabello sword. The bull slumped over as though someone had switched off the electric current. Miguel's banderillero cut both ears at the President's answering sign to the storm of handkerchiefs. The crowd wanted to give him more.

After the corrida was over we went to the pleasant crowded din of the old Maria Cristina Hotel in Algeciras. We had some time with Luis Miguel and Mary learned what he had said when he had dedicated the bull: "Mary and Ernesto: I dedicate the death of this bull to our friendship that lasts forever." We were both touched and it made things more complicated than ever. I was trying to be absolutely just in my appraisal of Luis Miguel and of Antonio but the rivalry was beginning to shape up like a civil war and neutrality was becoming increasingly difficult. Seeing what a great and vastly versatile matador Luis Miguel was and the perfect condition he was in I knew what Antonio was up against when they would begin to fight on the same programs.

Luis Miguel had his place to maintain. He claimed to be the number one bullfighter and he was rich. That was weight to carry in the ring but he really loved to fight bulls and he forgot about being rich when he was in the ring. But he wanted the odds in his favor and the odds were the tampering with the horns. He also wanted to be paid more money than Antonio per fight and that was where the deadliness came in. Antonio had the pride of the devil. He was convinced that he was a greater bullfighter than Luis Miguel and that he had been for a long time. He knew that he could be great no matter how the horns were. Luis Miguel was being paid more than Antonio was and I knew that if this occurred when they fought together Antonio would turn loose that strange molten quality he had inside himself until there would be no doubt in anyone's mind and especially Luis Miguel's who was the greater fighter. Antonio would do that or he would die and he was in no mood to die.

The trip to Ronda was beautiful climbing up through the mountains, instructive and very funny. Antonio was going to be given a gold-embroidered parade cape by his fan club in this famous town where he was born and he said he wanted to show me some things and tell me some things. I asked what he had to wear to the presentation of the cape.

"We just go as toreros," he said, which meant, in these days, a polo shirt with no tie. After the presentation and when Antonio had made his customary speech of, "Thank you very much," he turned to me and said, "Now you go to get yours."

"My what you——" I said.

"Your gold medal from the Mayor at the City Hall."

"Dressed like this?"

I had a gray jersey polo shirt that had been washed, fortunately, but would not button at the neck.

"It's a clean shirt," he said. "We're toreros, aren't we?"

We paraded through the streets accompanied by all his local followers in their best clothes. The medal was in honor of the centenary of Pedro Romero and had only been given by the city of Ronda to five other people. Antonio was delighted at the formal attire of the Mayor and dignitaries and our chulo appearance. Chulo is a double-meaning word for Sevillian underworld or picaresque characters. One meaning is quite rough.

It was a fine but exhausting day and we met and were entertained by Antonio's true good friends of that strange and lovely town. We left the cradle of bullfighting and stronghold of usury and climbed, circled and finally dropped down the narrow mountain road to follow a beautiful clear mountain stream down to the sea below Marbella where the coast road took us to Málaga. There we collected the mail at the lock box in the post office under the dusty trees, leafed through it and drove out of the city and up into the hills to the long wooded drive, some of the trees smashed by boulders brought down by a cloudburst the winter before, and through the great iron gates to the pebbled drive with the big and small dogs barking welcome, through the heavy door and into the cool marbled warmth of La Consula.

In five days Antonio and Luis Miguel were to fight together in the same ring for the first time since Luis Miguel had been wounded and retired in January seven years before in Bogotá, Colombia.

CHAPTER

7

The opening fight of the rivalry was in Zaragoza. Everybody who cared about bullfighting and could afford the trip was there. All the Madrid critics were there too and the Grand Hotel was jammed at lunch time with bull breeders, promoters, aristocracy, people with titles, ex-horse contractors and all of Antonio's small band of followers. There were a great many followers of Luis Miguel, politicians, officials and the military. Bill and I had lunched at a tavern he knew in the town and when we went up to Antonio's room we found him cheerful but a little detached. I could always tell when people were getting on his nerves by the way he moved his head as though his neck were a trifle stiff and by his Andalucian accent becoming a little more pronounced. He said he had slept well. After the fight we would all drive to Teruel and eat there. I said Bill and I would drive directly from the ring since Antonio would make better time in the Mercedes. All this reminded me too much of the conversation before the Aranjuez fight but

he wanted it that way. When we left he grinned naturally and winked once, as though we had a secret. He was
not nervous; but he was a little tense.

I stopped at Luis Miguel's room to wish him good
bulls. He was a little tense too.

It was a hot day and the June sun was heavy. Luis
Miguel's first bull came out well and charged the picadors strongly and with decision. Luis Miguel took him
on the first quite and showed the same good form, arrogance and domination with the cape that he had the last
time we had seen him. Then Antonio took the bull away
with the cape the next time he charged a picador. He
took him out into the ring and passed him so slowly, so
close, holding himself absolutely straight and sculptur-
ing each pass and slowing it and lengthening it until you
could not believe such cape work was possible. The
crowd, and Luis Miguel, knew that their difference with
the cape had been established.

Luis Miguel put in two good pairs of banderillas and
a final superb pair citing the bull and waiting for him
until the last fraction of a second before he swung to one
side, dropped the sticks in and then pivoted clear. He
was a beautiful banderillero.

With the muleta he took command of the bull quickly,
worked him intelligently and well with good long
passes. But there was no magic in it. Antonio's quite on
his own bull which was not too simple an animal had
taken something out of him. He went in to kill twice
with no luck and no great decision. Then he went in
better and half the sword was stiff in the high, hard,
death hole and Luis Miguel skillfully brought the bull's
head down to where it was muzzling the spread muleta
on the sand and drove in the point of the descabello
sword and it was over. The crowd was for him and he
made a round of the ring, thin-lipped and faintly smil-

ing. It was a look we were to get to know very well that summer.

Antonio's first bull came out well. Antonio took him and moved in with him closer and closer on each pass, adjusting himself to him and moving the cape with the old heart-stopping rhythm.

He kept the bull intact through his contact with the picadors and when the banderillas were in he took up where he had left off fighting perfectly at Aranjuez a month before. He had come back intact. The goring had not diminished him in any way. It had only taught him a lesson and he started the faena with all of his purity of style, making the bull his partner and helping him, lovingly, to pass the horn in as deadly a way as it could go and be controlled. Finally when the bull had given everything he had Antonio killed him with a single trip in over the horns. To me it was a touch low but it was all right with the public and the President. He cut the ear.

Bill and I relaxed. He was back the same as though he had never been away. That was the important thing. The pain and the shock had done nothing to him inside. He looked a little tired around the eyes. That was all.

Luis Miguel's second bull was weak in the legs. He tried to work him well. After a good start the bull lost a hoof. Miguel asked permission to pay for the substitute and fight him after Antonio's bull. Then he did away with the sad, broken-hoofed animal, and Antonio's last bull came out.

He was not truly brave, was a slow starter, and was not a bull for a spectacular faena. He needed to be dominated, cut down with the muleta and killed promptly. Instead Antonio started to work on him and make a bull out of him. He passed him beautifully with the cape, anticipating and correcting his defects with his courage and knowledge. It was beautiful to watch but very spooky. All the banderilleros were nervous and I watched Miguelillo's face white and drawn.

With the muleta Antonio figured he had him straightened out but when he cited him from well out the bull braked with his feet in the middle of the pass and tried for the body under the muleta. Antonio kept him in the muleta and got rid of him. The bull tried it again. He never had been a bull for the sort of work Antonio wanted to do. He knew it now and knew he had been overconfident with him. So he gave him the necessary passes to prepare him for killing, squared him up and went in over the horn with the sword up to the pommel in the slightly lower forward edge of the legal sticking hole.

Luis Miguel took the substitute, a large, slightly overweight bull from Samuel Flores with good horns and no bad intentions, and worked him in his style. He put in four pairs of banderillas; not the very expensive kind he had placed in his first bull but good ones from Macy's. With the muleta he was intelligent, sure and calm. Then he did all the tricks he knew the public loved and did them perfectly. The first time with the sword he went in with a little doubt. The second trip in he headed for the very top of the sticking place and got in a half a blade again, solid and perfectly placed in aorta country. He watched the bull go through his coronary and then turned the lights off with the descabello. They gave him both ears and the tail.

Bill said, "It's going to cost Luis Miguel a lot of money this season if he wants to have the last word with Antonio at forty thousand pesetas a time."

It was true that Luis Miguel had beaten him, on paper, but the draw of the bulls is luck, or is supposed to be, and on the two bulls Antonio had been ahead. The added bull made the day come out in Luis Miguel's favor.

"Today was very instructive," I said. "Luis Miguel is very intelligent and that quite of Antonio's on his bull got to him. That will stay with him. You'll see. That's what Antonio did to poor Aparicio in Madrid."

"He'll always fight after Luis Miguel, remember," Bill said. "That's a terrible advantage too."

"We'll have to keep track of the substitutes," I said. "We may see quite a lot of substitutes."

"I don't think it will last that long," Bill said.

"Neither do I," I agreed.

I was exhausted by the fight and by what we had seen and felt. I never liked to drive after a fight but we had bulls the next day at five o'clock at Alicante on the Mediterranean and the day after that at six o'clock in Barcelona and the day after that at five o'clock in Burgos. You have to see those distances on a contour map and know what the roads are like to know what that means. We had driven that day to Zaragoza from Madrid and before that we had driven up from Málaga to Madrid.

A big part of the road to Teruel had never been rebuilt properly since the Civil War. It was narrow, cut-up blacktop, dangerous to drive with any speed at night but it was the only way for us to cut through to the Mediterranean. We drove it in the dark as fast as it was safe, or a little faster, and all met at the Government hotel on the north side of Teruel. It was late but they made us a good meal of hors d'oeuvres, steaks, vegetables and salad.

"How do you feel?" I asked Antonio.

"Very good. The leg didn't bother me. I only felt a little tired toward the end. How do you feel?"

"I'm always tired after that kind of a fight."

"It takes me a while to cool out," he said. "I ate a ham sandwich and drank a glass of beer. But sometimes my stomach doesn't want it. This food's all right for this hour."

"Can you sleep now from here on?"

"Sure. I'll put the seat back and sleep to Alicante. It's better for me to ride at night and sleep in the daytime. If you sleep at night you can wake frightened. If you wake in the daytime you wake happy."

He laughed and we started to joke with the others. In principle we never talked about the fight at the late meal afterwards. We joked, sometimes quite roughly, and Charri, a rotund, hard-drinking Basque who was devoted to Antonio and followed all of his fights, had the old Shakespearian role of the Fool. He told very funny stories as well as serving as a butt for jokes. There were many things and people to joke about since the people who make a cult of bullfighting are only barely sane and those who are matador worshipers are even more vulnerable.

Sometime after midnight the three cars left to drive on to Alicante through the night and Bill and I left a call for daylight and were on the road in a cold thin fog that lay over the town and along the bed of the river until the sun rose and started to burn it off. We passed the places where the fighting had been and I did not try to explain the operation or the siege to Bill but only to point out various features of the terrain. With them in mind he could understand the fight from any sound account. The distances were all smaller, as usual, and the deadly cold and snow were gone. But I saw many places that could scare me still by their bare nakedness.

Seeing the terrain did not bring back the fight. That had never gone away. But it helped a little, as always, to purge some things that happen on the earth to see how little difference it has made to the dry hills that once were all-important to you. Riding along the road toward Segorbe that morning I thought how a bulldozer does more violence to a hill than the death of a brigade and that a brigade that was left to hold a height so that it, the brigade, might be destroyed, may enrich the soil for a short time and add some valuable mineral salts and a certain amount of metal to the hill but the metal is not in mineable quantities and any fertilization made will be washed away from the infertile soil in the rains of spring and fall and in the run-off of the snow of winter.

There were some other places I wanted to see since we would be going through them; places that I was sure I remembered incorrectly due to haste or stress or the distortions of vision that being under fire bring, but we would see them sooner or later and I could make my corrections of memory then. There were certain places that I liked to show to Bill for their incredibility; to show them as museum pieces of the impossible in war. But I had shown him the positions on the road above the village of Guadarrama on the way up to the pass on the high road to Avila and they had been so obviously preposterous to hold that I did not blame him for not believing me. When I saw them I could not believe them myself although the original memory of them was sharper than any photograph.

I was glad when we reached Segorbe, a very old, beautiful and unharmed town that I had been through many times but never had time to stop in. Bill had lived there one time with Annie and knew every place in town. We had a good breakfast of coffee, cheese and fruit and bought some fine walking sticks that the country people use in the mountains made of a wood that I had only seen before in Africa. We also bought some very good cherries and put them in the iced wine bag.

We came down out of the mountains and the hills past the steep, wildly confused, high-walled old gray Iberian town of Sagunto with its Roman and Moorish hodgepodge of conqueror-imposed buildings and its lovely medieval town. Sagunto from a distance always seems to be about to slip or slide like the slates on a steep roof that has been damaged and the upper part, when you are in it, seems to be held up by cactuses. I would have liked to stay and walk through it again and climb up to the castle but we had bulls in Alicante so we drove through the heavy Sunday traffic of cars, bicycles and motor scooters toward Valencia. The country was a rich coastal plain that ran from the sea to the foothills. We drove past the dark trunks and varying greens of orange and lemon trees and the silvery green of olive orchards and the houses were white and framed by palms and rows of cypresses. The country was so rich and so cut up that it all seemed to be gardened rather than cultivated. The road was jammed with Sunday drivers and the motor scooter accidents began to average about one every five to six miles.

We bypassed Valencia and took the coastal road outside the lagoon with the wild beach and the forest of umbrella pines on our left. The wind was blowing, and the sea would be breaking heavily on the beach. The slant-rigged boats were sailing on the lagoon and the green rice fields were moving in the wind. Far away across the lagoon was the white of the villages and the brown jagged hills. There were fishermen along the banks and in the cuts and many of the motor scooters carried fishing rods and gear. They were maintaining their rate of accidents. It slackened as we drew away from Valencia on the sea road to Alicante but picked up again as we came closer to that city.

The ride along the coast road was more dramatic and the coast bolder than that south of Málaga but heavy Sunday traffic cut the views of the blue sea breaking and creaming on the rocks below and it was good to get into the pleasant and booming town of Alicante. There was an excellent new hotel, the Carlton, and they gave us a comfortable cool room with a big balcony even though the town was in fair week and we had explained that we had to leave immediately after the bullfight.

Antonio was feeling good and looked very rested and confident. He had slept all the way to the hotel and then gone to bed and slept until noon. There was much business being done. The promoter for the Valencia ring was talking to Antonio about which bulls he wanted and we excused ourselves and went out. We were expecting Ed Hotchner who had flown to Madrid from New York but had arrived too late to make the Zaragoza fight and was arriving either by plane or by car.

Bill and I had lunch with Domingo and the Valencia promoter, who was a friend of mine, and the two promoters of the Alicante ring. They worked out the program for the Valencia fair. It was to be on a basis of Antonio and Luis Miguel and one fight would be a mano a mano between Luis Miguel and Antonio. "It ought to be a wonderful feria," Bill said.

Just then Hotch showed up freckled and indomitable and we got him something to eat. He'd had a rough ride in the taxi, and things had been balled up in general, but he put it behind him very fast when we told him we were all three going to watch the fight from the callejón.

"What do I do if the bull jumps into the callejón Papa?" he asked.

"You jump into the ring."

"What do I do when he comes back into the ring?"

"You jump back into the callejón."

"It's elementary," Hotch said. "It's no problem at all."

That afternoon four of the five bulls of Juan Pedro Domecq were excellent. Antonio was confident and happy with both of his and opened up his academy of how bulls should be fought with his first veronica and closed it with his last sword thrust. He cut both ears and the tail of the first bull and the ear of the fourth. Every move he made was perfect and classical. But it was not cold. He was loving with the bulls again and he directed them and commanded them with grace and elegance and he killed cleanly and perfectly. It was good to see him from so close in the callejón and to hear everything he said to the bulls and to his people as he fought this perfect fight.

After the fight we agreed to meet at Pepica's, the great open-air eating place at the Gran de Valencia just north of the port on the sandy beach. It was an all-night drive to Barcelona and one section of the road after we would enter Catalonia was really bad. The people at the hotel would not let us pay for the room. I met some friends of old friends and a couple of alive old friends as we were leaving in the car. They had seen us at the ring and come to say good-bye. I told them we would be back to Alicante on the way to the feria of Valencia on the twenty-third of the next month.

"And how did you come back to the bulls, Ernesto?" one old friend asked me.

"Antonio," I said.

"It was worth it," he said. "But otherwise it is a stinking mess."

"I'm making a recon," I said. "I'll know about it when I'm through."

"Well, good luck," he said. "Maybe I'll see you in Valencia. How many fights will Antonio have there?"

"Probably five."

"I'll see you there," he said.

We drove in the twilight and the dark on the crowded road where the holiday-makers were returning to their homes. There were fewer motor scooters on the road and almost no accidents and I decided that the less able had been eliminated in the earlier hours. They are not a very nocturnal vehicle anyway, and they turn in early.

Bill wanted to drive all of the time without relief. He enjoyed traffic and bicycles and all the unlighted vehicles made him happy. He did not like to play easy courses and he had read a rather silly and confused book about bullfighters and the hardships and horrors they went through in travelling from fight to fight. We all knew the author and had come to not care for him intensely but we had all assumed, mistakenly, that he had driven these barbarous distances himself. Bill rightly believed that if this unlikely character could drive these distances night after night and survive to write books about it then it should be easy for Bill who was a pitiless driver to surpass him. Hotch scenting and savoring a sporting event thought it was wonderful if Bill wanted to drive until he died. We could make a book on it.

"Aren't you sleepy at all Bill?" I asked. "We've been on the road and standing up in the callejón since six o'clock this morning."

"We sat down at lunch," Bill said.

"He's cheating," Hotch said. "We'll make him eat standing up."

"Should we stop and get some coffee?" I asked.

"I don't think it would be sporting," Hotch said. "If Bill is a horse we can't dope him."

"Do you think they'll give him a saliva test at Pepica's?"

"I don't know what installations they have," Hotch said. "I've never eaten at Pepica's. But I certainly think they ought to have a saliva test in a town the size of Valencia."

"It's only at the Port of Valencia," Bill said somberly.

"Cheer up, Bill," Hotch said. "We'll run a proper test in Barcelona."

Dinner at Pepica's was wonderful. It was a big, clean, open-air place and everything was cooked in plain sight. You could pick out what you wanted to have grilled or broiled and the seafood and the Valencian rice dishes were the best on the beach. Everyone felt good after the fight and we were all hungry and ate well. The place was run by a family and everyone knew everyone else. You could hear the sea breaking on the beach and the lights shone on the wet sand. We drank sangria, red wine with fresh orange and lemon juice in it, served in big pitchers and ate local sausages to start with, fresh tuna, fresh prawns, and crisp fried octopus tentacles that tasted like lobster. Then some ate steaks and others roasted or grilled chicken with saffron yellow rice with pimentos and clams in it. It was a very moderate meal by Valencian standards and the woman who owned the place was worried that we would go away hungry. Nobody talked about bullfighting. It was 382 kilometers to Barcelona and when we left the restaurant I told Antonio we would probably stop and sleep somewhere along the road and meet him at the hotel.

In the car Bill was very wide awake and said he was good for all night. He said the food had waked him up instead of making him sleepy. I suggested we stop at Benicarlo up the coast about 130 kilometers. Bill said he would pull off the road if he felt at all sleepy and he would stop at Benicarlo if we wanted to but that it was not necessary at all. I went to sleep at once and when I woke we were past Benicarlo and coming up on Vinaroz. It was a half an hour or so to daylight so we stopped at an all-night truck drivers' tavern and had sandwiches of slabs of cheese and I sliced raw onion for mine and we drank coffee and tried the local wine with some all-night types who were still drunk from the Vinaroz fiesta of Sunday. The ear some novillero had cut and the horns of the bull were behind the bar. They were good-sized

horns and no one had cut them down. The cool air along
the sea had made me very hungry and I wanted to see the
next piece of the country which I had last looked at on
the day the Nationalist army cut through to the sea and
we had nearly been trapped. So we waited for daylight
and drove across the lower Ebro at Amposta before the
sun was up.

The day was starting ugly with a wind and mist from
the sea. The road was very bad and the country was sad
in the gray light. The Ebro that had meant as much to
us at one time as the Marne or the Aisne looked equally
unhistoric. It was brown, though, as always, and the
current was heavy.

The day was starting sad for me but I tried not to pass
it on and we were in Barcelona at the big friendly hotel
in time to have had a good sleep if we were bullfighters
and could sleep in the daylight.

8

Outside the window a half-gale was whipping the branches of the plane trees and it was raining intermittently. It looked as though they might have to suspend the bullfight. But the advance sale had been big and I knew they would go on with it unless the sand was too wet to fight on at the hour fixed for the corrida. Bill would not try to sleep but went out to get the papers. I tried to take a nap but could not. It did not matter with me because I'd had a good sleep in the car after midnight. But I was worried about Bill and his wanting to do all the driving. I looked up Miguelillo, the sword handler, and he said Antonio was sleeping soundly.

When I saw Antonio he was disgusted with the weather but very eager for the fight to go on. He was anxious for his second chance at Luis Miguel. He said his leg hadn't bothered him at all at Alicante.

"What a good time and what a good meal we had at Pepica's," he said. "True, Bill?"

"True," Bill said.

"How is Bill holding up?"

"My Bill is a horse," I said.

It was a strong fight on a wild day and both Luis Miguel and Antonio were wonderful. Antonio Bienvenida was the senior matador and he nerved himself up to do a little good cape work, smiled his joyless smile that always looked as though it had two formal movements: gritting the teeth and then pulling back the lips to expose the dental structure. His bulls, they were all Sepulveda de Yeltes, were difficult and all he succeeded in doing with them was making them look more difficult.

Luis Miguel had drawn the best two bulls of the lot and he was superb with them both. He knew he could not compete with Antonio in the veronicas but he tried and did as well as I had ever seen him. When he put the cape behind his back and made the graceful Mexican passes of Gaona he was perfect. He put in three pairs of banderillas on each bull in his finest style and his work with the muleta was skillful, gallant and beautiful and close enough to give the feeling of the nearness of tragedy within the marvellous security. He killed one bull fairly well and his last bull perfectly and cut both ears and the tail. The crowd was wild about him and he deserved all the ovation.

Antonio had won the crowd with his beautiful cape work in a quite on Bienvenida's first bull. It was a bull that would not pass unless you made him pass. He made the bull look as though he did not have a fault.

In his own first bull, the third of the fight, it started to rain suddenly and heavily. The bull was good at the start and Antonio adjusted his timing to him exactly; moving always into the bull and swinging the heavy rain-soaked cape with delicate, calculated slowness just ahead of the bull's speed as the ring dampened and slowed. The bull was not really brave and his courage and his willingness to charge lessened under the down-pour. Antonio built him up with the muleta and took possession of him. But the bull was only good for a few beautiful right-handed passes and when he saw he had run out of bull in the rainstorm Antonio worked him into position and killed him promptly.

The rain had stopped during the fourth bull. Now on the last bull the crowd was still in a state of great excitement after Luis Miguel's triumph; that talking like a rustling stir that does not die down until the door swings open and the next bull comes in.

I watched the bull. Then I watched Antonio watching him and thinking. Juan, his brother, picked him up with the trailing point of the cape and the bull followed. I did not like him. I knew that but I could not instantly know why. Antonio knew all about him when he saw him make three moves and he knew what he was up against. But he went out to take the bull and by moving in on him provoked the charge and then, gaining a little ground on the bull each time, he measured his speed with the cape, waiting out the bull's cautiousness and controlling it into a measured rhythm as he brought the horns by closer and closer and closer on each pass, until he placed him where he wanted him, turned him on himself, and walked away.

When the bull charged the picadors all his faults were visible for anyone to see. Miguel had drawn two good bulls and been superb. Antonio had drawn two even better bulls the day before and had been wonderful. Those two could always be great with fine animals to work with. They were in a class where that meant nothing. But now Antonio had a bull that was showing he was hesitant in charging and that would have to be worked in a terrain that was supremely dangerous to get him to charge at all and then be controlled absolutely by the movement of the cloth so that he never broke off from it to try to gore the man.

Antonio went out and took the bull over on the bull's terms. If he had to work where it was deadly dangerous to work he would work there; but knowingly; not from ignorance. If he had to go way inside the bull's terrain and control him by the slow suavity of his moving the muleta so at that speed the bull's eye could never leave it, nor would it ever be speeded out of his vision by any desire of the man to shorten the long moment of true danger, he would do it. If he had to surpass Luis Miguel by keeping his absolute Bach-like purity of style and timing, doing it with this faulty instrument, he would do it. If he were killed it meant absolutely nothing to him at all at this moment.

So he did it, molding the bull, instructing him and finally making him like it and cooperate. The murmuring started in the crowd and then the shouting began on each incredibly beautiful pass. Then Antonio was doing it all to music and keeping it as pure as mathematics and as warm, as exciting and as stirring as love. I knew he loved bulls and I knew he understood them as a scientist. This was an impossible faena to do with the bull he had been given and I had seen a hundred variations of what matadors would do to rid themselves more or less honorably of a bull like this one. He had to surpass Luis Miguel and this was what he had been given to do it with. So he did it.

Finally he killed, going in perfectly and hitting bone twice; then burying the sword in to the red pommel guard. They gave him one ear although the crowd asked for both. But he had hit bone twice.

They carried them both out on the shoulders of the crowd and that was Barcelona.

Up at the hotel Antonio, tired more from the carrying

on the shoulders than from the fight, smiled his dark, happy smile as he lay on the bed under the sheet.

"Contento Ernesto?" he asked.

"Muy contento."

"So am I," he said. "You saw how he was? You saw everything about him?"

"I think so," I said.

"Let's eat at Fraga."

"Good."

"Be careful on the road."

"See you in Fraga," I said.

Luis Miguel was in another hotel and the crowds were so thick outside our own hotel that I could not get over to congratulate him. The crowds jammed the entrances to both hotels and for the first time it was like the great old days.

We got out of the city finally against the heavy returning traffic of the people who had spent the double holiday of Sunday and St. Peter's day in the country and drove in the glare of the oncoming lights on the dark wet road across Catalonia and into Aragon. The outfit caught up with us at Fraga, a lovely old town hung like a Tibetan city above the river that would have been worth the whole trip to see. But all we could see was a rainy street and a big zinc bar where the truckers stopped. The dining room above it was closed and their liquor wasn't good. We got an imperial quart of good Gibraltar whiskey from the car and all had whiskey and mineral water against the cold, wet night. We had two drinks apiece while they found us some fair tenderloin and cooked some eggs and brought a soup.

Antonio was happy but tired. He hated being carried on people's shoulders and it had opened the wound. We ate quickly but cheerfully. It was like a team that had won a big game but know they have to play tomorrow.

We talked over the best place to stop and everyone agreed the hunting lodge at Bujaraloz was the best.

"Do you want me to dress the wound?" I asked Antonio.

"No. It's nothing. Miguelillo taped it up tight. You can look at it tomorrow."

"Get a good sleep."

"I will. The road is good from now on. How are you?"

"Fine. Muy contento."

He grinned. "Make Bill sleep," he said. "Even if he is a horse you have to take care of your horse."

"We just give him some oats."

"Make him sleep," he said. "And sleep yourself. See you at Burgos."

When we were through Zaragoza and out in the flat country making good time along the highway with the Ebro on our right with its white badland hills and then, beyond them, the first mountains of Navarre, the day began to clear although the big mountains of the Iberian range on our left were still covered with cloud.

After Logroño, when we had left off skirting Navarre and gone through the edge of the vine country of the Rioja, we climbed up through the foothills of the Sierra de la Demandada through wild heaths and stunted oak trees and from the highest point looked down on the plateau of Old Castille with far below the poplar tree-lined road that led to Burgos.

It is always a shock to enter Burgos. It could be any town down in the hollow in the hills until you see the gray of the cathedral towers and then you are in it suddenly. We were there for bulls so I took the impact that the weight of its stone and its history made on me and Bill left to find a place to park the car in the crowd-jammed streets of the feria and I went up to find the outfit.

I saw Joni, Ferrer and Juan, the banderilleros, outside the hotel. Ferrer and Juan had come from the sorteo. They said the bulls looked good. We had drawn the best pair, they thought. Everybody felt good but tired. The cuadrilla had made a really rough trip from Barcelona but morale was good. They had hired out to be tough and this four-day swing was only practice for how it would be in August and September.

Antonio was fine. He had slept well in the car and at the hotel.

It was a very good fight although the Cobaleda bulls were difficult and dangerous. Antonio had one bull that could only be worked on the right. His left horn hunted the matador like a chopping sickle. So Antonio worked him beautifully with his right hand and killed him well.

His second bull was difficult too but he rebuilt him the way he had the bull in Barcelona the day before. He was as fine as always with the cape, did a beautiful classic faena and killed very well, putting the sword in way high. They gave him both ears. His work could not have been better and he never let the bull's difficulties show at all.

After the fight we drove to Madrid and got there in time to eat late at the Callejón. Bill had made the whole trip unrelieved at the wheel. We tried to count the number of mountain ranges we had crossed and figure the mileage we had made and then we gave it up. It did not matter. It was made.

On the evening of July second Annie and Mary showed up from Málaga, having driven it in one day just to show us. We drifted back into the edges of civilization and family life for two days and then took off for Pam-

plona via Burgos. We stopped at Burgos to see a corrida
of Miuras. They were the best and finest bulls we saw all
season, one was the noblest and most complete bull I had
seen in many years. He did everything but help the
puntillero to put the dagger in him when he was down.
We slept at Vitoria and drove on to Pamplona for the
feria of San Fermin.

9

PAMPLONA IS NO PLACE TO BRING YOUR WIFE. THE ODDS ARE
all in favor of her getting ill, hurt or wounded or at least
jostled and wine squirted over her, or of losing her;
maybe all three. If anybody could do Pamplona success-
fully it would be Carmen and Antonio but Antonio
would not bring her. It's a man's fiesta and women at it
make trouble, never intentionally of course, but they
nearly always make or have trouble. I wrote a book on
this once. Of course if she can talk Spanish so she knows
she is being joked with and not insulted, if she can drink
wine all day and all night and dance with any groups of
strangers who invite her, if she does not mind things
being spilled on her, if she adores continual noise and
music and loves fireworks, especially those that fall close
to her or burn her clothes, if she thinks it is sound and
logical to see how close you can come to being killed by
bulls for fun and for free, if she doesn't catch cold when
she is rained on and appreciates dust, likes disorder and
irregular meals and never needs to sleep and still keeps

clean and neat without running water; then bring her. You'll probably lose her to a better man than you.

Pamplona was rough as always, overcrowded with tourists and characters, but with a hard core of all that is finest in Navarre. For a week we averaged something over three hours sleep a night to the pounding of the war drums of Navarre, the piping of the old tunes and the dancers swirling and leaping. I've written Pamplona once and for keeps. It is all there as it always was except forty thousand tourists have been added. There were not twenty tourists when I first went there nearly four decades ago. Now on some days they say there are close to a hundred thousand in the town.

Antonio had to fight on July fifth in Toulouse but he turned up for the first encierro on the seventh. He had wanted to fight at Pamplona but there had been a mixup with the contracts when he changed management at the start of the season and went with the Dominguín brothers. He loves the fiesta and wanted us to do it together and we did it all right. We did it for five days and nights. Then he had to go to Puerto de Santa Maria to fight Benitez Cubrera bulls on July twelfth with Luis Miguel and Mondeño. It was the only time all year that Luis Miguel outclassed him in the ring when they fought together.

Afterwards I asked him. He said Luis Miguel had drawn the better bulls but he had not been up to the form that had held in every fight all season.

"We didn't really train at Pamplona," I said.

"Maybe we didn't train exactly as we should," he agreed.

We had not really gone there to train but the program had not included his being gored and getting a horn wound in the right calf from a Pablo Romero bull in the early morning running and paying no attention to it after it was dressed and he was given anti-tetanus. He had danced all night to keep it from stiffening and then run again the next morning to show his Pamplona friends he was not refusing the fights because he did not like the bulls. He never looked at the wound and he would not go to the bull ring surgeon because he did not want to have anyone think he gave it any importance and he did not want to worry Carmen. When I noticed it was suppurating a little later George Saviers, a doctor friend of ours from Sun Valley, cleaned it and dressed it properly and kept it clean until Antonio went off to fight at Puerto de Santa Maria with it still open.

Actually, at the Puerto, I learned from friends, Luis Miguel had two ideal and perfect bulls and fought them beautifully and then did all the tricks including kissing one bull on the face. Antonio had two worthless bulls, the second very dangerous. He had no luck killing on the first but on the second and very bad bull he got everything out of him he could, killed excellently and was given the ear. But it was Luis Miguel's day all the way.

I stayed at Pamplona because by that time Mary had a very painful broken toe from slipping on a stone when we were swimming up on the Irati. She walked with a stick with pain and difficulty. The fiesta had been a little wild perhaps. On the first night Antonio and I had noticed a very chic-looking small French car with a beautiful girl in it accompanied by what turned out to be a Frenchman when Antonio jumped up on the hood of the car to bring it to a stop. Pepé Dominguín was along and when the occupants of the car got out we informed the Frenchman that he could leave but the girl was our prisoner. We would also keep the car as we were short of transport. The Frenchman was very affable. It turned out the girl was American and he was only guiding her to her lodging where her friend was waiting. We said we would attend to all that and "Vive la France et les pommes de terre frites."

Bill, who knew every street in Pamplona, found the girl's friend, who was even more beautiful than the original prisoner, if that was possible, and we all moved off into the night on the dark flagged narrow streets of the old town where Antonio knew a place he wanted us to go to sing and dance. Eventually we gave the prisoners their parole and they arrived fresh, lovely and well groomed at Choko's Bar in the morning as the first drums and dancers were going by on their way to the Plaza and they stayed good and loyal and lovely prisoners through the feria of Valencia at the end of the month.

Turning up with a couple of prisoners is sometimes ill-received in marital circles but these prisoners were so lovely and so good and so adaptable, cheerful and happy in their prisonerhood that not a wife but favored them with her approval and even Carmen believed us when she met them at her and my joint birthday party at the Consula on July twenty-first.

In the meantime we had found out how to beat the erosion of the fiesta and get away from the noise that was getting on the nerves of some of the more valued members of our group. It was to leave in the forenoon and drive up the Irati River above Aoiz and picnic and swim and then drive back in time for the bullfights. Each day we drove further up that lovely trout stream into the great virgin forest of the Irati that was unchanged since the time of the Druids. I had expected it would all be cut and destroyed but it was still the last great forest of the Middle Ages with its great beeches and its centuries-old carpet of moss that was softer and lovelier to lie on than anything in the world. And each day we went farther and farther into it, getting back later to the fights until, finally, we skipped the final fight, the novillada, and penetrated to a place I will give no details on because we want to go back there again and not find fifty cars or jeeps have found it. By the forest road we could make our way to nearly all the places we had to hike or pack into at the time I wrote about in *The Sun Also Rises* although you would still have to walk and climb from the Irati to Roncevalles.

Finding the country unspoiled and being able to have it again and share it with the people that were together that July I was as happy as I had ever been and all the overcrowding and the modernizations at Pamplona meant nothing. In Pamplona we had our old secret places like Marceliano's where we went in the morning to eat and drink and sing after the encierro; Marceliano's where the wood of the tables and the stairs is as clean and scrubbed as the teak decks of a yacht except that the tables are honorably wine-spilled. The wine was as good as when you were twenty-one, and the food as marvellous as always. There were the same songs and good new ones that cracked and suddenly pounded onto the drums and the pipes. The faces that were young once were old as mine but everyone remembered how we were. The eyes had not changed and nobody was fat. No mouths were bitter no matter what the eyes had seen. Bitter lines around the mouth are the first sign of defeat. Nobody was defeated.

Our public life was at the Bar Choko under the arcade outside the hotel Juanito Quintana used to own. It was at this bar that a young American journalist let me know that he would have liked to have been at Pamplona with us thirty years ago, "when you used to go into the country and know the people, when you used to know the Spaniards and care about them and their country and about writing and not waste your time sitting in a bar seeking adulation, making wise cracks with your sycophants and signing autographs." There was a lot more of it and it was all in a letter he had written because I had reamed him out for not picking up some tickets I had bought for him from an old scalper friend who worked all the ferias. He was in his early twenties and he would have been as square in the nineteen twenties as he was in the end of the fifties. He did not know that it is always there and you can find it and his handsome young face already showed the traced lines of bitterness around the upper lips as he tried to straighten me out on Pamplona. It was all there and he had been invited to it; but he could not see it.

"Why do you waste time on that creep?" Hotch said.

"He's not a creep," I said. "He's a future editor of the *Reader's Digest.*"

Pamplona was a good time and afterwards Antonio fought twice in Mont de Marsan in France where he was wonderful but the bulls were with altered horns so he never even talked about the fights with me. After the last fight he flew down to Málaga for the birthday party Mary had organized for Carmen and me. It was quite a party and I might not have noticed I was sixty if Mary had not made it so important and so pleasant. But that party drove it in.

We had been getting increasingly lighthearted, in the best sense of the word, since we started the training when Antonio threw away the stick after the grave cornada of Aranjuez. We had spoken about death without being morbid about it and I had told Antonio what I thought about it which is worthless since none of us knows anything about it. I could be sincerely disrespectful of it and sometimes impart this disrespect to others, but I was not dealing with it at this time. Antonio gave it out at least twice a day, sometimes for every day in the week, travelling long distances to do it. Each day he deliberately provoked the danger of it to himself, and prolonged that danger past the limits it could normally be endured, by his style of fighting. He could only fight as he did by having perfect nerves and never worrying. For his way of fighting, without tricks, depended on understanding the danger and controlling it by the way he adjusted himself to the bull's speed, or lack of it, and his control of the bull by his wrist which was governed by his muscles, his nerves, his reflexes, his eyes, his knowledge, his instinct and his courage.

If there was anything wrong with his reflexes he could not fight in this way. If his courage ever failed for the smallest fraction of a second the spell would be broken and he would be tossed or gored. In addition he had the wind to contend with which could expose him to the bull and kill him capriciously at any time.

He knew all these things coldly and completely and our problem was to reduce the time that he had to think about them to the minimum necessary for him to prepare himself to face them before entering the ring. This was Antonio's regular appointment with death that we had to face each day. Any man can face death but to be committed to bring it as close as possible while performing certain classic movements and do this again and again and again and then deal it out yourself with a sword to an animal weighing half a ton which you love is more complicated than just facing death. It is facing your performance as a creative artist each day and your necessity to function as a skillful killer. Antonio had to kill quickly and mercifully and still give the bull one full chance at him when he crossed over the horn at least twice a day.

Everyone in bullfighting helps everyone else in bullfighting in the ring. In spite of all rivalries and hatreds it is the closest brotherhood there is. Only bullfighters know the risks they run and what the bull can do with his horns to their bodies and their minds. The ones who have no true vocation for bullfighting have to sleep with the bull every night. But nobody can help a bullfighter immediately before the fight; so we tried to cut the time of acute anxiety down. I prefer the term anguish, controlled anguish, to anxiety.

Antonio always prayed in the room before the fight at the last when the well-wishers and the followers were gone. If there was time at the ring nearly everyone slipped into the chapel to pray once before the paseo. Antonio knew I prayed for him and never for myself. I was not fighting and I had quit praying for myself during the Spanish Civil War when I saw the terrible things that happened to other people and I felt that to pray for oneself was selfish and egotistical. In case my prayers were invalid, as they well might have been, and to make sure someone competent was doing it I took out a membership in the Jesuit Seminary Fund Association at New Orleans for Carmen and Antonio. There was a class graduating who, when they were ordained, would pray for them each day.

So we cut the time of thinking about it to the minimum and we were lighthearted in all the time between the fighting and the immediate preparation before going to the ring. Pamplona was lighthearted enough. The party back at La Consula was even more so. One of the attractions Mary had set up in the park was a shooting booth she had hired from a travelling carnival. Antonio had been a little shocked in 1956 when Mario, the Italian chauffeur, had held up cigarettes in his hand in a gale of wind for me to cut off their lighted ends with a .22 rifle. At the party Antonio held cigarettes in his mouth for me to shoot the ashes off. We did this seven times with the shooting gallery's tiny rifles and at the end he was puffing the cigarettes down to see how short he could make them.

Finally he said, "Ernesto, we've gone as far as we can go. The last one just brushed my lips."

I quit while I was still ahead and refused to shoot at George Saviers because he was the only doctor in the house and the party was just underway. It went a long way. Three days later we had made the trip up the coast and were at Valencia for the first fight of the feria.

10

Valencia was very hot and all the hotels were crowded. There were no rooms at the Royal although our reservations had been confirmed at Alicante and we settled the outfit into the fine, old, dark, cool Victoria as fast as rooms could be available and using the big air-conditioned bar at the Royal as a point of rendezvous. The heat was hard on the girls and we taught them the different ways to walk across the town using the narrow cross streets and the high buildings for shade.

The first corrida was a modified disaster. The Pablo Romero bulls, beautiful and huge as always, were mostly bad in the legs or went to pieces fast. Antonio Bien-venida could do nothing with his first bull which was a trotter who stayed on the defensive. Bienvenida went on the defensive too and they out defended one another until he stuck the animal defensively and it was dragged out. I hoped that General Buck Lanham who had flown over for the birthday and this feria did not think that this was bullfighting. He had his no comment face on.

Luis Miguel's first bull started out fast, brave and powerful and Luis Miguel gave him the full treatment from the large cambiado with both knees on the sand through the three pairs of banderillas close to the fence. Two of the pairs were beautifully done and I saw Buck was with it now. Banderillas are the easiest thing for a spectator to appreciate, if not evaluate, and Luis Miguel always did them as though he were explaining them step by step and you could watch him make the steps with his own feet. Then with the muleta the bull began to as-phyxiate with the heat and his over-weight and after a few good passes he ran out of breath and slipped into the defensive and then torpidity. Luis Miguel got rid of him with a skillfully placed half sword blade.

Jaime Ostos was enormously brave with the third bull which was enormously stupid and without temperament but with just enough tendency to probe with his right horn to make him dangerous on that side. Jaime got everything he could out of him with his left hand and had no luck while going in twice with the sword. Finally he killed well.

Luis Miguel drew a really good second bull and did everything with him that we had seen him do in Algeciras when he was at his very best. I think with this bull he reached his high point of the fair. He could not do anything more perfect in his style. The bull lost part of a hoof at the start of the work with the muleta but strangely did not go lame and Luis Miguel led him through five long series of passes each one bringing a shouted response from the crowd. With the music play-ing he did a second half that was as emotional as the first. Then he did all the tricks and finally killed cleanly, high and beautifully with no tricks at all.

He had done everything that he could and done it perfectly and his triumph was complete and absolute.

He made two turns around the ring with his tight-lipped smile that was becoming sad lately. He was not arrogant but seemed to be thinking about something else as he held the two ears up and his cuadrilla followed behind him throwing back the women's bags, shoes, flowers and the wine skins and straw hats. They kept the cigars. There was a great empty space on the sunny side of the ring that the country people in their black smocks and dusty berets had not come in to fill and I wondered if that was what Miguel was thinking of as he passed with his sad face or whether he was wondering what he could do more than he had done that day when he and Antonio would fight together and the chips would all be down.

The second day with Antonio Ordóñez, Curro Giron and Jaime Ostos there were even more vacancies in the sunny side and the ring was only a little more than half full. The heat was as bad as the day before and there was a heavy wind blowing from Africa. Antonio did not care or think about the half filled ring once he was out on the sand. He had scratched that when he came into the ring and cased the house. Since he had been fighting somebody else had always made the money and it was no tragedy although he wanted it badly and knew how hard it was to come by in this trade, how hard to keep and how much he and Carmen needed it for the simple and decent plans they had.

In this fight there were only two good bulls. Antonio's first bull was worthless. We were watching from the red planks when his second bull came out. He was good, fast, well armed, sound all around, good on this side as Juan trailed the cape, good on the other as Ferrer tried him. Antonio ran out with the cape saying to Ferrer, "Out." He wanted to be alone with the bull and then he cited him and when he came in a rush Antonio coupled into him to make the long, slow endless passes that were like some deep music that only he and the bull could hear. He could always break my heart with the cape since I had first seen him in Pamplona six years before and today he was greater than ever. He had watched Luis Miguel the day before and he was showing the public and himself and us and history what Miguel would have to beat to win.

He changed to the banderillas after only one pic to keep this bull completely intact and carefully watched Joni and Ferrer place the sticks. Then he took his sword and went out to the bull.

He took possession of him and lowered his head with four low passes on one knee and then did the finest, most erect, most beautiful, complete and classical faena with the muleta I had ever seen him make until then. It had everything beautiful that he had ever done before but it had the beautiful flow of the water as it curves over the crest of a dam or a falls. It was all of one piece and every pass was sculptured. The crowd started with the murmuring noise and then finally was roaring like a rapids so that the brass of the music was drowned out. It was like all of his great faenas and it was better than any. The unbelievable thing was that he made it on a windy day.

When he finished the work with the muleta Antonio went in to kill four times; each time going in for the high death notch perfectly and hitting bone. Then he drove the sword in finally lying on the bull as his sword went in and the bull came out dead under the thrust of his hand. They gave him the ear although he had gone in to kill four times because each entry when he hit bone was equivalent in danger to a kill. What they would have given him if he had not hit bone on the first trip in no one can say.

It was a big night at Pepica's on the beach. The surf was pounding in. We were all happy and nobody was cooled out after the emotion of the fight. We were like a happy tribe after a successful raid or a great killing. The pitchers of sangria went fast and we did not have to eat early as we usually did because of Antonio. He had left to drive to Tudela in Navarre to fight the next day with Luis Miguel and Ostos. Ordinarily we got Antonio to bed by midnight. The serious training had started again the day after the party. We had regular hours and customs again.

Luis Miguel had fought that day in Palma de Mallorca and I was glad he had not seen what Antonio had done that day. It would have worried him. I was fond of him but from what I had seen in Valencia I was sure he could not win in what was going on.

It was obvious now that it took both Antonio's and Luis Miguel's names to fill a bull ring at the huge price for tickets they were forcing the promoters to ask. If something happened to either one they would smash the whole basket of golden eggs. But something was going to happen. I was never surer of anything ever and I was quite sure that Antonio was certain too. In the night I wondered how things were with Carmen because she was the best, the straightest and the most loyal and intelligent of all of us who were involved in this death and money business. She could not win all the way no matter how it went. I was glad I had some people praying for her that had some authority.

In the fourth fight at Valencia Antonio and Luis Miguel met in the ring for the fifth time that season. The bulls were Samuel Flores. Gregorio Sánchez was the third matador. It was a cloudy day with heavy oppressive heat. The ring was sold out for the first time in the feria. Luis Miguel's first bull was hesitant, braked in the center of the charges and kept trying to slip into the defensive. Miguel worked on him carefully and intelligently. The bull kept dropping his muzzle into the sand and Miguel worked to get it up and prepare the bull to take the sword. It was a bull that could give any bullfighter a bad time. But Miguel killed him promptly and skillfully on his second try. It was not what the public had paid to see but there was nothing else to give them and the best part of the public knew it and applauded. Miguel went out and saluted once and came back tight-lipped to the fence.

Antonio's bull came out and he took him over with the cape and made the same slow, straight, beautiful long passes that he did all season on every bull that would charge. They were not something that he made rarely or with an exceptional bull. They were his standard cape work on every bull that could be forced to charge and each time he tried to better them and make them closer and slower.

Luis Miguel put the cape over his back and did a fine series of Gaona's old passes in his turn to take the bull away from the horses.

With the muleta Antonio did a faena that was the equal of a wonderful one he had made in his first fight at Valencia. It had even more merit because this bull was not as good as the other and he had to cradle him and hold him more with the muleta. I watched him from the fence as he moved the bull, always completely controlled, never letting the horn touch the cloth but swinging it just at the bull's speed as he turned him a half-circle, another half-circle, winding the bull around himself, and then he turned him a complete full circle as the crowd shouted at each pass. I watched Miguel's face too. There was no expression on it.

Antonio killed finally when he had done every beautiful, classic and truly dangerous pass that could be made with a bull and then bettered them all again. The crowd gave him a great ovation and the President gave him both ears.

Luis Miguel went all out to win in his second bull and

took him on both knees with the beautiful one-handed swinging pass with the cape that is called the larga cambiada. It is spectacular and beautiful but is nowhere near as dangerous as passing the bull slowly by with the cape held in both hands. The crowd loved it though, and rightly, and Luis Miguel was a master of it.

In banderillas he was superb. One pair that he put in was unbelievable. The bull waited for him close to the fence, his flanks heaving, blood streaming down one shoulder from the pic wounds, and his eyes watching Miguel who walked in to him slowly, his arms spread wide, the harpoon pointed sticks held straight forward. Miguel walked past the point where he should cite the bull and make him charge, then past the point where this way of putting in the sticks was still safe, then past the point where it was possible with the bull still watching him to be sure of catching him. Then the bull charged at three paces and Miguel feinted with his body to the left and as the bull's head followed him brought the sticks down and pivoted on them to come out over the opposite horn.

He took the bull with the muleta close to the planks of the fence and passed him with right-handed passes. I could hear what he said to the bull, hear the bull breathe and the clatter of the banderillas as he passed under the muleta past Miguel's chest. The bull had only been pic-ed once, but deeply. His neck muscles were strong and Miguel was making him throw his head high to tire them and bring the head down for killing. But the bull was bleeding badly and losing force.

Miguel took great care of him and passed him gently when he took him out from the fence but he was losing him fast. He ran down like a phonograph record finally and when he would not play Miguel played with him. He stroked his horn and leaned his arm on his forehead and pretended to talk to him on a telephone. The bull could never have answered but he could answer even less now that he was bled out and winded and unable to charge. Miguel led him through a few tentative moves holding his horn to help him concentrate and then he kissed him.

Now he had done everything he could do with this bull except propose honorable matrimony and all he had to do was kill him. He had lost him at the same time he had won him with the banderillas. But it had not shown at the time.

The bull had no charge in him to help Miguel with the sword. He would have to go in hard and high and slam it in if he were to compete with Antonio now. He could not do it. He went in five times but he could not slam in. He was not hitting bone. He simply could not bring himself to drive in. The crowd was strangely silent. They were watching something happen to a man that they could not understand.

I thought Antonio had killed him off with the cape and the muleta and I was sorry for him. Then I remembered the trouble he'd had in Tudela where he'd been hit by a bottle and that perhaps that was working in his sub-conscious and making a block that kept him from going in with the sword the way a shooter gets a flinch. But he could not go in to kill properly anymore and he tried five times and then, with the bull bleeding out and his head hanging, he brought the muzzle down a little lower, with his muleta spread on the sand, jabbed him in the neck with the descabello sword and turned the current off.

Antonio drew a bull that there was nothing to be done with. He proved it to himself and anyone else would have been gored or demoralized in the proving. Then he killed it promptly.

That evening after the fight Antonio, up in the room,

lying on the bed under the sheet after his shower asked, "How does it look to you?"

"We've got him," I said.

"You were content?"

"*Socio*," I said, which means partner. We called each other this to skip emotion.

"Tomorrow I have a surprise," he said.

"What?"

"A little picnic on the beach by the sea."

"Let's eat early and get to bed tonight."

Whatever it was that makes people not worry in the times between combat there was plenty of it around that summer and it did not come in bottles although the pitchers of sangria were cold and beaded over quickly in the hot dry wind that blew all day and all night. We were all happy that the big fight was coming and we ate big, delicious sole fresh from the sea or *rouget* that the Spaniards call salmonete and a saffron paella with many sorts of seafood and shellfish in it. We had eaten a fresh green salad to start and for dessert we ate melons. The season had been late but they were prime now and on the way back to town there was the mighty wonder of the fireworks. This night all the crashing of massed brasses and the booming drums turned to light and then weeping willow trees of light were blossoming in the sky with thunderclaps until the Northern Lights burst over the avenue of the fair and it was over with the whisk of falling sticks in the dark before the lights came on.

I do not know what Luis Miguel did nor how he slept the night before the first decisive fight at Valencia. People told me he had stayed up very late but they always say things after something has happened. One thing I knew; that he was worrying about the fight and we were not. I did not bother Miguel nor ask any questions because he knew I was in Antonio's camp now. We were

still good friends but since I had seen his work and studied him with different types of bulls I was convinced he
was a great bullfighter and Antonio was an all-time great
fighter. I was convinced that if Antonio did not attack
too hard he and Miguel could make a lot of money if they
cut their prices and each was paid the same. If Antonio
was not'paid the same he would increase the pace until,
if Miguel tried to equal him or surpass him he would be
killed or wounded so badly he could not keep on
fighting. Antonio, I knew, was ruthless and had a strange
implacable pride that had nothing to do with egotism.
There were many things behind it and it had a dark side.

Luis Miguel had the pride of the devil and a feeling of
absolute superiority that was justified in many things.
He had said so long that he was the best that he really
believed it. He had to believe it to go on. It was not just
something he believed. It was his belief. Now Antonio
had gravely wounded his confidence and he had come
back entire from a disastrous goring to do it and had
done it every time but one that they had fought together.
The relief for Luis Miguel had been that there had always been a third matador fighting with them so the
comparison could not be absolute. Luis Miguel could
always be better than the third man. Now he would have
to be in there with Antonio alone. It was no place to be
for any bullfighter the way Antonio was going and still
less a place to be if you were receiving more money than
he was. Antonio was going like a river in flood and he
had been going that way all year and all the year before.

That was how things added up the morning of the day
before the fight when I went out for a walk around the
lovely old town in the early morning. We took a chance
on how to spend the day and the chance paid off. We
spent it at a fine, old, simple country house and hunting
lodge about thirty miles out from town on the orange-

growing land that lies between the sea and the big rice-growing lagoon of the Albufera where, in winter, they have some of the greatest duck shooting in the world. When you reached the beach through the orange groves and then the forest of umbrella pines it stretched for five white miles of sand without a house. The wind was still blowing strongly and there was a heavy surf running.

It was a wild, wonderful day on the beach and we swam all day when we were not eating or playing football. In the middle of the afternoon we decided not to go to the bullfight and were going to have a ceremonial fire and burn all the tickets. Then we decided that might be bad luck so we played some more football and then swam until dusk, going far out past the surf and then having to swim in against a strong current that was running to sea to the westward. Everyone was dead tired and we all went to bed early like worn-out healthy savages.

Antonio slept happily and well and woke happy and rested. I had just come from the sorting out of the bulls. They were good-looking bulls with real horns from Ignacio Sánchez and Baltazar Iban. The lots were even. The wind had risen in the night and the day was overcast. It was blowing half a gale outside and it was more like a fall storm than the end of July.

"Are you stiff?" I asked him.

"Not at all."

"Are your feet all right?"

My own right foot was swollen from dribbling and kicking barefoot.

"They're all right. I never felt better. How's the day?"

"Lots of wind," I said. "Too much."

"Maybe it will go down," he said.

It did not go down and by the time the bullfight started and Luis Miguel's first bull came into the arena the sky was dark with storm, there was no sun, and it was blowing a full gale. I had been in to see Luis Miguel before the fight to wish him luck. He had been smiling and friendly as always with his same old charm he showed each day when I looked in on him. But both he and Antonio had been deadly serious as they crossed the sand of the ring in the paseo and came up to the fence after saluting the President.

Luis Miguel's first bull came out fast and good. He was well shaped and big enough but not overfed and had good, useful horns. He charged the horses with power and looked as though he would be a fine bull for Miguel to work with. But after the banderillas were in he began to fade. Miguel tried to work him in the lee of the fence but the bull did not like it there. Miguel took him further out and the muleta was blowing flat out in the gusts. Miguel worked him skillfully waiting out his half-charges and dominating him intelligently. He got some good passes out of him and killed him fairly promptly. He went in all right but I could see he was still having trouble doing it. The mechanism in him that was damaged had not been repaired yet. But it held up enough for him to kill this bull promptly.

Antonio's first bull was more difficult than Miguel's. He was powerful, well-armed and well built but he was hesitant and had a tendency to break off his charges. Antonio moved way in on him with the cape and started to make a bull out of him wind or no wind. With the muleta he found what lee he could in the shelter the planks of the barrera made and made the bull like it there by the way he moved in on him constantly exposing himself. The bull began to light up and with Antonio forcing him and not letting his attention flag or die he wound him around in low left-hand passes and lifted him past his chest in beautiful pases de pecho. He linked it all together, always making the bull believe and keeping him in his exact rhythm. It was an excellent faena with all his slowness and grace. Then he squared the bull up very exactly, furled, sighted, and slammed in hard to kill. The bull went down almost as though he had been shot. The point of entry was a touch off of the high death notch but they gave him the ear and he circled the ring with it. He had won the first round.

Luis Miguel's second bull was from the ranch of Baltazar Iban which had been substituted by the veterinaries for one of the two Ignacio Sánchez bulls that had been refused for inadequate horns. This bull started off well and Luis Miguel was excellent with the cape. He was attacking hard and was determined to surpass Antonio. But when it came time for the banderillas the crowd wanted Luis Miguel to put them in himself and he refused. I could not understand this as, to me, it was the best thing that he did in all his long and varied repertory. Whether it was pride and wanting to beat Antonio at his own game or something he felt about the bull, who showed symptoms of slowing up, I did not know. The public were very disappointed.

Miguel seemed to be right, for the bull faded fast but not before Miguel had made an excellent faena with the muleta starting with a statuesque right-handed pass and following with a series of naturales, good low left-handed turning passes that, given the difficulties of the wind and the state of the bull, were admirable. Then came a few Manolete tricks and he had his public all back with him. All he had to do was kill now to cut an ear. But he had the same trouble trying to slam in. The mechanism was not working again and he went in with the sword four times before he killed the bull. He was way behind now and it was getting darker and the wind was rising. The big sprinkling tank came out to wet down the blowing sand and no one talked much in the callejón during the intermission.

We were all suffering for the two matadors and the test they were being put to by the storm.

"It's inhuman for them both," Domingo, Luis Miguel's brother, said to me.

"And it's getting worse."

"They'll have to put the lights on," Pepé, the other brother, said. "It will be dark after this bull."

Miguelillo was wetting the fighting cape Antonio would use so it would be heavier in the wind.

"It's barbarous," he said to me. "What a barbarous wind. But he's strong. He can do it."

I moved down along the fence.

"I don't know what's the matter with me with the sword," Luis Miguel said, leaning on the barrera. "I'm awful with it." He looked detached and spoke as though he were commenting on someone else or some phenomenon that puzzled him. "There's one left. Maybe it will be all right with the one that's left."

Some friends were talking to him and he was looking out at the ring without listening. Antonio was looking at nothing and thinking about the wind. I stood with him leaning on the barrera and we did not say anything.

After the intermission Antonio's bull came in. He was black, well built, had good horns, and looked stupid. He did not follow the capes with any interest and when Antonio brought him up to Salas, the picador, he charged the horse but broke away quickly each time when the pic hurt him. The sobresaliente or substitute who would have to kill the bulls if Luis Miguel and Antonio were both gored asked permission to make a quite and the bull promptly caught him and tossed him. Antonio rescued him with his cape. His trousers were ripped by the horn and he'd lost a shoe. Juan picked it off the sand and tossed it over the fence.

The bull was worse after the banderillas and wanted no part of anything. Antonio had to hold the muleta like a sail in the wind to work him and chop him into position for killing. He had to do it all with sheer force of wrists for the muleta, spread by the sword, blew like a sail. I knew he had a bad right wrist for years and it was always taped before the fight so it would not buckle on him when he killed. Now he was paying no attention to it but it slipped a little as he went in to kill and the sword did not go in straight. As he came in to the barrera after killing he stood by me. His face was drawn and taut and his wrist hung like a pitcher's dead arm. The lights came on and I saw a wild look in his eyes that I had never seen before in the ring or out. He started to say something and then stopped.

"What is it?" I asked.

He shook his head and looked out to where the mules were dragging the bull out. Under the lights the wind was already blowing the furrowed sand that had been watered down barely a quarter of an hour before.

"Ernesto, this wind is terrible," he said in a hard, strange voice. I had never heard his voice change in the ring except with anger and then it was lower, never higher. This was not higher either nor complaining. He wanted to establish something. We both knew something was going to happen but this was the only moment when we did not know who it was going to happen to. It lasted only long enough to say the five words. He took a glass of water from Miguelillo and spat it out on the sand and reached for his heavy fighting cape without favoring his wrist.

Luis Miguel's last bull came in under the lights in a rush. He was big with good horns and he was fast. He

chased a banderillero over the fence and smashed at the
burladero and splintered the planks with his left horn.
He tried to jump the fence but did not make it. When the
picadors came in he charged well and knocked over the
horse. Luis Miguel was secure but discreet with the cape.
The wind showed his basic weakness in veronicas and
made the gay passes with the cape over his shoulders
impossible. The bull was nervous and had a slight tendency to check himself and brake with his hind legs and
Miguel did not want to put in banderillas. The crowd
was even more insistent than they had been on his second bull, but he refused. The crowd did not like it. One
of the things they paid the big prices for was to see him
place banderillas. He was losing the crowd but believed
he could straighten out the bull with the muleta and do
a good faena that would bring them back. He picked
himself the least windy place he could find in the ring
where this bull was workable, close to the planks of the
barrera, and went out with a heavily watered and mud-
died muleta. He called for more water and scuffed the
red serge cloth in the sand to give it more weight.

The bull came well and he gave him two statuesque
passes holding the sword and muleta in both hands, the
bull passing his whole length under the cloth as Miguel
lifted it. He saw he did not own the bull yet so he made
four low right-handed passes to punish him and take him
over. Then he took him out away from the lee of the
planks since the bull was getting disillusioned there
Luis Miguel made two more right-hand passes and the
bull seemed good now. Then as he had started a third
pass the wind blew the muleta up and uncovered him
and the bull reached under the cloth and seemed to catch
him in the belly with his right horn. He went up in the
air and the bull's other horn caught him in the crotch
and threw him on his back. Antonio was racing with the

cape to take the bull away but before anyone could reach him the bull had three chops at Miguel as he lay on his back on the sand and I saw clearly the right horn go into his groin.

Antonio had the bull now and Domingo, who had jumped the fence the moment Luis Miguel was hit, was dragging Luis Miguel clear. Domingo and Pepé and the banderilleros lifted him and rushed him toward the barrera. We all lifted him over and we ran through the callejón and out through the gate under the stands and down the corridor to the operating room. I was holding his head up. Luis Miguel held his hands on the wound and Domingo was pressing down with his thumb above the wound. There was no hemorrhage and we knew the horn had not hit the femoral artery.

Luis Miguel was completely calm and very gentle and courteous with everyone.

"Thank you very much, Ernesto," he said when I was holding his head up and then cushioning it while we undressed him and Dr. Tamames cut away the trousers at the wound. There was only one wound. It was right at the top of the thigh in the right groin. It was circular, about two inches across and was blue at the edges. Now, with Miguel lying on his back, the bleeding was all internal.

"Look, Manolo," Luis Miguel said to Dr. Tamames. He put his finger on a spot just above the wound. "It goes in here and then goes up like this in here."

He traced the course of the trajectory of the horn on his groin and his lower abdomen. "I could feel it go in."

"Muchas gracias," Tamames said, harsh and matter of fact. "I'll find out where it went."

The infirmary was like a bake oven, there was no air and everyone was sweating. Photographers were climbing all over, flashes were going off and newspaper reporters and curious people were crowding in at the doors.

"We're going to operate now," Tamames said. "Get these people out of here, Ernesto, and," he said very low to me, "get out yourself."

Miguel was comfortable on the table now and I told him I'd be back.

"Until then, Ernesto," he said, and smiled. His face was gray and sweating and his smile was loving and gentle. There was a pair of Guardia Civil at the door and another pair outside.

"Clear all these people out," I said. "No one is to come in. Then put a pair on the door and keep the door open so there will be some air."

I had no right to give orders but they did not know that and they were waiting for orders. They saluted and started to clear the operating room. I walked out slowly and as soon as I was under the stands sprinted for the entrance to the callejón. Overhead there was a roar that broke again and again and as I came out to the red fence of the barrera under the yellow lights Antonio was passing a big red bull closer and slower and more beautifully than I had ever seen him move a cape before.

He kept the bull entire and only permitted a single pic. The bull was very fast and strong and carried his head high. Antonio wanted him fast and he could not wait until the banderillas were in. The bull was really brave and he was confident he could bring his head down properly. He did not care about the wind now nor about anything else. He had a really brave bull for once in the feria. It was the last bull and nothing could spoil it. What he was going to do with it would stay with the people who saw it all their lives.

He dedicated the bull to Juan Luis at whose house in

the country we had spent the day before and threw the hat to him and grinned. Then he did everything with the bull that the greatest matador could do and did it better. He started off with Miguel's two-handed passes never moving his feet, purifying the line of the pass and bringing the bull high up into the air under the soft sweep of the muleta. It would be impossible for the horns to pass him closer. Then he switched to naturales, low, beautiful, slow left-handed passes and wrapped the bull around him again and again and again. At every pass the crowd exploded.

After he had shown how slow and beautifully he could work he moved way in on him and started to show how close and how dangerously he could make him pass. He went past reason and seemed to be fighting in a controlled rage. It was wonderful but he had gone way past the impossible and was doing consistently and continually what no one could do and doing it happily and lighthearted. I wanted him to stop it and kill. But he was drunk with it and he had done all this in the same piece of terrain he had selected and every series of passes was linked to every other series and every pass to every pass.

Finally he squared the bull up as though he hated to say good-bye to him, furled the muleta and slammed in. He hit bone and the sword bent under the shock. I was worried about his wrist but he lined the bull up again, furled and slammed in high again. The sword went in up to the hilt and he stood in front of the red bull with his hand up and watched it with no expression on his face until it fell over dead.

They gave him both ears and when he came up to the barrera to get his hat Juan Luis shouted to him in English, "Too much."

"How's Miguel?" he asked me.

Word had come through from the infirmary that the cornada had penetrated the abdominal muscles and had laid open the peritoneum but had not gone into the intestines. Luis Miguel was still under the anaesthetic.

"It's okay," I said. "It didn't perforate. He's still asleep."

"I'll get dressed and we'll go to see him," he said. The crowd was in the ring rushing at him to carry him out and he was pushing them away. But there were too many of them and they finally hoisted him on their shoulders. From the white-washed three-bed hospital of the bull ring, which was as hot as a prison cell in Senegal, they took Luis Miguel on a stretcher to his air-conditioned room at the Royal to fly him to Madrid early the next morning. Antonio and I had gone to see him at the ring as soon as Antonio was dressed.

"All three of us matadors slept in here one night when I was a novillero," Antonio said. "It was as hot as this."

Luis Miguel was weak and tired but in good spirits when we saw him in the hospital at the ring and we left at once in order not to tire him. He joked about me giving orders to the Guardia Civil and Domingo said that when he came out of the anaesthetic the first thing he said was, "What a man Ernesto would be if he could only write." Three days later we were all to be together again in the Sanatoria Ruber in Madrid with Antonio in bed on the third floor and Luis Miguel on the first. Fifteen days later they fought their second mano a mano in Málaga. That was the way it was that year.

The next morning the group that had been together since Pamplona broke up. It was sad and nobody wanted to do it. Antonio was fighting in Palma de Mallorca the next day and the day after in Málaga. The rest of us headed for Alicante, then through date palms and the rich, crowded, flat farming and fruit country of Murcia, past Lorca, to break out and up into the wild mountain country and along the lonely valleys with the white-washed houses of the villages and the herds of sheep and goats raising the dust along the road until we came down out of the hills in the dark past the entry to the ravine where they had shot Federico Garcia Lorca and saw the lights of Granada. We slept in Granada and it was cool and fresh at the Alhambra in the early morning and we were at La Consula in time to eat before the bullfight down in Málaga.

Next morning when Bill and I went into Málaga we learned Antonio had been wounded at Palma de Mallorca. He had been caught and gored in the right thigh but had finished his work with the muleta brilliantly, gone in to kill well and they had given him the ear. They had flown him to Madrid after the fight.

We tried to get a call through to Madrid but there was a five-hour or more delay. There was no space on the plane to Madrid that evening and no sure space in the morning. I had a strong hunch the wound was worse than it sounded and Bill said, "If you're worried, why don't we drive up after lunch. After all, we do know the road now."

So I wired Carmen we would be there in the morning and sent messages from all of us. Bill's theory was that Spanish roads in spite of the dangerous curves and drops and the four mountain ranges we had to cross were safer to drive at night because there was almost no cart traffic and no herds on the roads and almost no private cars. The big trucks that hauled fish from the Mediterranean to the capital and the other night truckers were all skillful drivers and reasonable and helpful with their lights.

We usually tried to drive in daylight because we both loved to see the country but the night theory was sound and we made Madrid in time to get something to eat and sleep and be out at the hospital by the time Antonio would be awake.

Antonio was resting easy. He was happy to see us and very cheerful.

"I knew you'd come," he said. "Before Carmen got the wire I was sure."

"How is it?"

"It's deeper than they thought and it goes further up into the muscle than I thought. The bad thing for healing is that it went into the scar of an old wound. Right in the center."

"What were you doing?"

"It's always your own fault. But I was right."

"Wind?"

"Yes but in a different ring."

He did not want to talk about it; only the technical details of the wound and how soon it would heal.

"Take it easy," I said. "I'll talk to Manolo and Carmen and come by and see you in the afternoon."

"Let me send a message to Miguel. I'll write it and Carmen can lower it down outside the window on a string."

Carmen was so happy and relieved that Antonio had a simple wound and that her brother had been lucky with his and was coming along well that she was as cheerful, outwardly, as she had been at our birthday.

Antonio wrote the message and Carmen and Miguelillo, the sword handler, put it on a string attached to a bottle opener and lowered it down to Miguel's window. It read, E. Hemingway the writer asks respectfully if LM. Dominguín the bullfighter will consent to receive him. It came back up with the answer Yes with great pleasure if A. Ordóñez the bullfighter is not afraid he might catch the hives from L.M.D. by this contact.

Luis Miguel was fine and very cheerful and affectionate. His wife was beautiful, calm, and charming. I thought he had lost all of whatever it was that was weighing on his mind and had thought things through and had his old confidence back. He was not worried now and Antonio's being wounded too had cheered him up.

The nine fights of the Málaga feria had been based on Luis Miguel and Antonio so they had to patch the card up as well as they could. But the shadow of Luis Miguel and Antonio was over the feria and all of the matadors were out to beat them even in their absence. Perhaps it was the best place to pick to beat them.

The start of Hemingway's sixtieth birthday celebration, July 21, 1959, at noon beside the Davises' pool. Bill Davis is seated at left, Hemingway stands talking to Gianfranco Ivancich, and General Buck Lanham sits with Dr. George Saviers of Sun Valley, Idaho, at right. Mary Hemingway sits near the pool talking with Señora Ivancich and Mrs. Saviers. Photo by Cano.

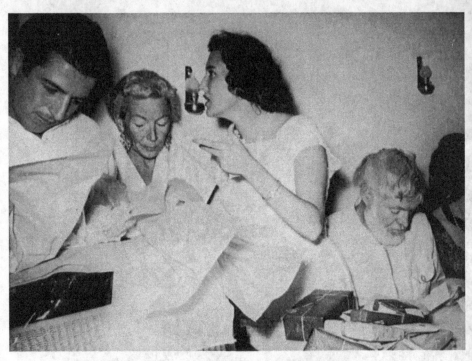

Opening presents later that night: Antonio Ordóñez, Mary Hemingway, Carmen Ordóñez (whose birthday was also being celebrated), Ernest Hemingway. Photo by Cano.

At the portable shooting gallery Mary Hemingway hired for the party, Ernest Hemingway shoots a lighted cigarette from Antonio Ordóñez's lips. Buck Lanham watches in the foreground. Photo by A. E. Hotchner.

Hemingway with a drink during the 1959 Pamplona feria. Photo by Cano, courtesy the John F. Kennedy Library.

Hemingway at Bar Choko with A. E. Hotchner and Mary Schoonmaker, one of the "prisoners" the group took during the Pamplona feria. Photo courtesy A. E. Hotchner.

On the beach at Málaga. Photo by A. E. Hotchner.

Dominguín being tossed by his third bull during the Málaga mano a mano with Ordóñez. Photo © Larry Burrows.

A. E. Hotchner preparing to appear as the sobresaliente for the mano a mano between Ordóñez and Dominguín at Ciudad Real. Hemingway, Bill Davis, and Ordóñez look on. Photo by Larry Burrows, LIFE Magazine © 1960 Time Inc.

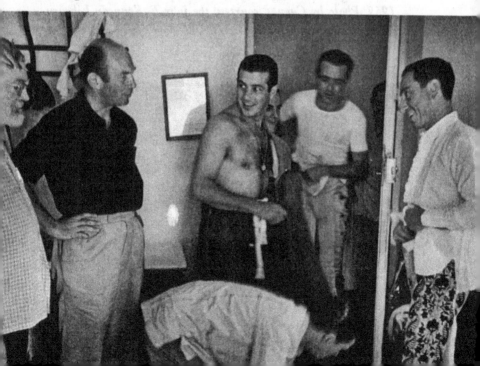

*Luis Miguel Dominguín performs a pase natural, Bayona,
1959. Photo by Cuevas, courtesy the John F. Kennedy Library.*

Antonio Ordóñez performing a remate at the end of a series of veronicas, Sevilla, 1959. Photo by Cuevas, courtesy the John F. Kennedy Library.

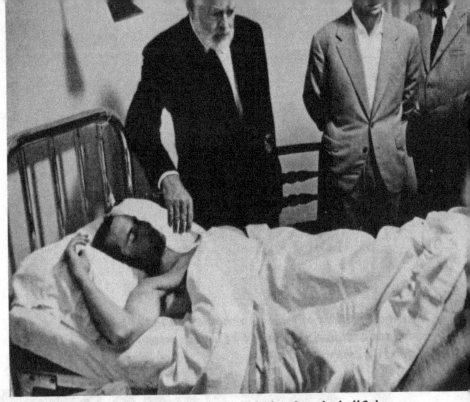

Hemingway at Dominguín's bedside after the bullfighter was gored at Bilbao. Bill Davis stands at right. Photo © Larry Burrows.

Hemingway and Ordóñez confer at ringside, Bayona, 1959. Photo by Fournol, courtesy the John F. Kennedy Library.

CHAPTER

11

IT WAS PLEASANT TO HAVE THE MÁLAGA FAIR OVER AND TO
be quiet at La Consula again. Each evening at the end of
the fight we had walked from the ring, or sometimes took
a horse-drawn carriage to the Miramar Hotel where the
bar and terraces that looked out on the sea were crowded
with summer people, the rich of the town and a mixture
of bullfight fans, followers, fighters, managers, breeders,
journalists, tourists, beats, summer perverts of all sexes,
acquaintances, friends, nobility, shady characters, smug-
glers from Tangiers, nice people in jeans, un-nice people
in same, old friends, ex-old friends, drink cadgers and
characters. It was nothing like the lovely healthy though
strenuous life of Pamplona and our homely life of Valencia but it was interesting and funny up to a point. I
only drank Campanas that the bartender kept cold in a
bucket of ice behind the bar and when the conversation
reached the decibels of the bird house in a zoo we would
go and watch a pair of kids that we knew dance down on
the planked floor on the lower level where the packed

tables stretched out toward the sea. But it was a relief when it was over and a great pleasure not to have people asking you or more often telling you about something that you had seen but did not want to talk about nor explain.

Antonio was out of the hospital. He had gone to Luis Miguel's ranch to train in the ring there. We heard nothing except that the next fight was on for the fourteenth of August if Luis Miguel was in shape and Antonio was coming down to train at La Consula before the fight.

Antonio turned up three days before the fight with his friend Ignacio Angulo, a very pleasant Basque about his own age, whom we called Natcho. Antonio said the leg did not bother him at all but that the wound in the scar tissue had healed slower than normal. He could not wait for the next mano a mano with Luis Miguel but he did not want to think about it nor about bullfighting, nor to talk about them. He knew how good the day on the beach had been for him before the Valencia fight and we took up where we had left off there. Then, after gay, carefree lunches and the long pleasant dinners and the good sleeping that came from swimming, it was suddenly the day before the fight. Nobody had mentioned the fight until Antonio said, "Tomorrow I'll dress in town at the hotel."

It was one of the very greatest bullfights I have ever seen; Luis Miguel and Antonio both came to it as the most serious thing in their lives. Luis Miguel had gone through his grave wound in Valencia and the wound, and how lucky it turned out, had given him back his confidence that Antonio's unbelievably perfect work and his lionlike rush and courage had impaired. Antonio's being gored in Palma de Mallorca had proven that he was not invulnerable and it was lucky for Luis Miguel that he had not seen Antonio's work with the last bull of the fight at Valencia. I cannot truly think that he would have wanted any more of him if he had. Luis Miguel did not need the money although he loved money and what it bought very much. More than anything it was important to him to believe he was the greatest matador alive. He no longer was but he was the second greatest and on this day he was very great indeed.

Antonio came to the fight with all the confidence he had in Valencia. What had happened in Mallorca meant nothing to him. He had made a small mistake that he did not wish to discuss with me and he would not make it again. He had been sure for a long time that he was a better matador than Luis Miguel. He had proved it last in Valencia and he could not wait to prove it again on this day.

The bulls were from the ranch of Juan Pedro Domecq and none of them looked different except the first. There were two though that could have been difficult for any other matadors but Luis Miguel and Antonio. Luis Miguel was pale and gaunt and tired-looking when he took his first bull. The bull was dangerous and chopping both ways with his horns. Luis Miguel dominated him with tired grace. It was not a bull he could be brilliant with but he handled him with intelligence and skill and made what passes the condition of the bull would permit. When he killed him he went in solidly but the sword slid in sideways and the point showed out through the hide behind the bull's shoulders. A banderillero pulled the sword out with a swing of his cape and Luis Miguel killed the bull with the descabello on his first attempt. Watching from the fence I was worried about how Miguel looked and I hoped he was sound with the sword again. This one had been an accident but it made me worry.

Another thing that worried me was the many photographers and motion picture men present who had no previous bull ring experience. Any movement while the matador is working the bull that the bull can see may distract him and make him charge, thus breaking the matador's control of him with the cloth without his knowing why it has happened. Everybody in the callejón knows this and is careful at all times to keep their heads below the fence level when moving and to remain absolutely still whenever the bull is facing them. A conscienceless or criminal bullfighter leaning against the fence inside the ring could attract the bull's attention by an involuntary-looking flick of the cape and launch him on another fighter who was preparing to go in to kill.

Antonio's first bull came out and he took him with the cape as though he were inventing bullfighting and it was going to be absolutely perfect from the start. It was how he fought all summer. That day in Málaga he surpassed himself again and he made poetry of movement with the hunting, seeking, pressing mass of the bull. Then, with the muleta, he sculptured his passes gently and slowly making the whole long faena a poem. He killed him with a single estocada going in perfectly and the point of entry of the sword an inch and a half down from the top of the death notch. They gave him both ears and the crowd asked for the tail.

Luis Miguel's second bull came out trotting and I thought what bad luck he has now that it has turned. It was hard to make the bull stand still long enough to charge the horses, and the pics he took did not steady him. I felt worse and worse for Miguel who was taking it without complaint. He could not run to put in banderillas but he directed exactly how he wanted them placed. They steadied the bull down a little.

Luis Miguel took him with slow, two-handed, low passes and began his education with the muleta. He stopped his trotting tendency and held him so he would charge from one place and then follow the cloth at the rhythm that he created for the bull. He passed him high and under the cloth and then he commenced to work him with low, soft, swinging naturales with the sword in his right hand slanted out from his hip.

Tall, straight and unsmiling, unmoving from the terrain where he had elected to work the bull, Luis Miguel adjusted the muleta to the normal level of the bull's eyes so that he would not cramp his neck and commenced to swing him around him in the sort of naturales that Joselito would have signed. He finished off with a beautiful pase de pecho, the left-handed pass that brought the bull's horns past his chest and let the folds of the muleta sweep down the bull's body from his horns to his tail. He squared the bull up, furled the muleta on its stick, sighted high up and went in perfectly with all he had. It was the third bull of the fight to be killed by a single sword thrust. Miguel had fought him beautifully and had to make him in order to fight him. He had the sword back now and all his confidence with it. He came in with a deprecating smile and took the two ears and the tail modestly and circled the ring with them. I noticed that Miguel was favoring his right foot a little where his first bull had stepped on him but he was not concealing it. I knew his right leg hurt him and he did not feel completely solid with it. He was being wonderful and I never admired him more.

I did not think Antonio could be better with the cape than he had been in his first bull. But he was. As I watched him from the fence I tried to think how he could do it and do it always and make it so beautiful and moving. It was the closeness and the slowness that carved the figure and made each pass seem permanent. But it was the complete naturalness and the classic simplicity as he

watched the death go by him as though he were oversee-
ing it and helping it and making it his partner all in one
ascending rhythm that made it so moving.

With the muleta, this time, he started out with the four
great low passes he used with the right knee and leg
extended on the sand to take command of the bull. Each
pass was a model in execution but it was not cold work.
It was done so close that the horns passed at millimeters
from his thighs or his chest at every pass. There was no
leaning against the bull's body after the horn had gone
by. There were no tricks and every pass was a long pause
in the breathing of the people who watched the man and
the bull. I was never afraid for Antonio with the cape
and I did not have any worry in all this wonderful faena
although each pass was the most truly difficult and dangerous for a man to make in bullfighting. The bull was
good, much better than Miguel's had been. Antonio was
happy with him and he made a perfect, beautiful and
deeply moving faena. He did not let it go on too long and
he went in perfectly to kill his friend with a single estocada.

Four bulls were now dead from one sword thrust each
and the fight had been one long crescendo. They gave
Antonio both ears, the tail and cut a lower leg with hoof
attached. He circled the ring as happy and unpreoc-
cupied as though we were at the pool. The crowd wanted
him to take one more ovation and he asked Luis Miguel
and Don Juan Pedro Domecq, who had bred the bulls,
to go out with him.

It was up to Luis Miguel now. He took his bull on both
knees with a larga cambiada letting the bull almost reach
him with the horn before he swung him clear with the
cape. This bull was good and Luis Miguel made the most
of him. He was well pic-ed and Luis Miguel had the
banderillas put in rapidly. At the fence I thought he

looked very tired but he was paying no attention to his physical condition, absolutely avoiding any limping and was fighting with the same passion as though he were a hungry boy beginning his career.

With the muleta he had the bull placed a little out from the fence and jamming his back against the planks and sitting on the estribo, the strip of wood that runs around the inner side of the barrera to give the fighters a toe-up to vault it, he passed the bull five times past his outstretched right arm that signalled the bull's way with the outspread red cloth. The bull went by each time with a whoosh of heavy breath and with a clatter of banderillas, his hooves heavy on the sand, his horn passing close to Miguel's arms. It looked suicidal but with a good bull that charged straight it was only a fairly dangerous trick.

After this Miguel took him out into the ring and commenced to do classic passes with his left hand. He looked tired but confident and he was working well. He made two series of eight naturales in beautiful style and then on a right-hand pass with the bull coming at him from the rear the bull had him. From where I was leaning on the fence the horn seemed to go into his body and the bull tossed him a good six feet or more into the air. His arms and legs were spread wide, the sword and muleta were thrown clear and he fell on his head. The bull stepped on him trying to get the horn into him and missed him twice. Everybody was in with their capes spread and this time it was his brother Pepé, who had vaulted the barrera, who dragged Miguel free.

He was up in an instant. The horn had not gone in but had passed between his legs to toss him and there was no wound.

Miguel paid no attention to what the bull had done to him and waving everyone away went on with his faena. He repeated the pass on which the bull had caught him and then repeated it again as though to teach both himself and the bull a lesson. He went on to make other passes mathematically close and correct, giving no importance to anything the bull had done to him. He made the passes more emotional and a little trickier. The public liked them better. But he fought cleanly and well and did none of the telephone tricks. Then he killed well, slamming in as though he had never had any trouble with the sword in his life. They gave him everything as they had to Antonio and he deserved it. When he had made his tour of the ring, and it was impossible to dissimulate his limp now that the leg had stiffened, he called Antonio out to salute the crowd with him in the center of the ring. The President ordered the bull to be given a tour of the ring too.

Five bulls were dead from five sword thrusts when the final bull came out and the noise from the crowd was silenced when Antonio moved way into him with the cape and commenced the long, slow magic passes. The crowd was shouting now on each pass.

The bull seemed to come out limping a little from under the pic although it was well placed. I think he hurt one forefoot slightly pushing against the pic while he was trying to get at the horse through the heavy protector. This lameness cleared up, or loosened up at least, when Ferrer and Joni placed the banderillas but when Antonio took the bull with the muleta he was still a little uncertain in his charges and had a tendency to brake with his front hooves instead of charging clearly through.

Leaning on the planks of the fence I watched Antonio work this out. He took the short charge from close to the bull and then lengthened it suavely. He got the bull moving with the slow movement of his muleta and, holding him in the cloth, extended his charges almost imperceptibly until he was finally charging the scarlet serge cloth from a good distance and passing well. None of this showed to the crowd. They only saw an animal that was hesitant and reluctant to charge change into an animal that charged perfectly and seemed exceedingly brave. They did not know that if Antonio had simply worked in front of the bull's face and tried to show them that the bull would not pass, as most matadors do, the bull never would have passed and the matador would have had to do half-passes or chops. Instead he taught him to charge well and to pass him completely with the horns. He taught him to do the truly dangerous thing and then controlled it and prolonged it with the magic control of his arm and wrist until he was making the same beautiful sculptured passes with this bull that he had made with the two others that were easy for him to work with. Nothing of this showed and after he had done all the great passes with this bull and made them with the same purity of line and emotion of their closeness and their ordered danger the public thought he had merely drawn another great and noble animal.

He made a perfect, emotional faena with this bull, holding him controlled in the long, slow passes in any one of which, if he had hurried or been even a shade abrupt, the bull would have broken in his charge and left the cloth to gore him. This way of fighting is the most dangerous in the world and on this last bull he gave an entire course in how to do it.

There was only one thing for him left to do. He had to kill absolutely perfectly; taking no advantage to himself; not dropping the point of entry of the sword just a touch, or a bare suggestion to one side, where it would still pass but have less risk of hitting bone. So when he furled the muleta and sighted with the sword, he aimed for the very high top of the notch between the shoulder blades and drove in over the horn, his left hand low and guiding with the cloth. He and the bull formed one solid mass and when he came out over the horn the bull had the long steel death in him to the hilt and the aorta was severed. Antonio watched him go down in a foot-gripping, staggering, rolling crash and the second mano a mano was over.

There was still the hysteria of the crowd, the ears, the tail, the hoof, the tour of the ring by the bull, the triumphal trip of both matadors and the chief herdsman of Domecq who had brought the bulls from ranch to ring, now carried on the shoulders of the crowd to the Miramar Hotel. There were the postmortems, the empty, purged feeling after a great fight, the things we said to each other, the dinner that night at La Consula, and in the morning early we were off in a chartered plane to repeat it all, with luck, at the Bayonne ring in France. The statistics had gone ahead by telegram and radio; ten ears, four tails, two hooves. But these meant nothing. What was important was that the two brothers-in-law had fought an almost perfect bullfight that had been unmarred by any tricks by the men or shady maneuvers by the managers or promoters.

12

THE FLIGHT FROM MÁLAGA OVER THE MOUNTAINS AND THE plateau of La Mancha and Castille was beautiful in the early morning and seeing the many steep and broken ranges made me appreciate what a road it was to drive. Before we had set down at Madrid and cleared for France there was a time when I could not appreciate the yellow country with its stripes of roads and brown towns as I should because the pilot and co-pilot let Luis Miguel and Antonio take their places. Neither one had a pilot's license then, as far as I knew, and I do not know in what other country this could happen. The theory evidently was that a bullfighter can do anything and I sweated out the variations in altitude and the sudden eccentricities of the aircraft looking down at the now unfriendly ground until the pilot took over.

The airport at Biarritz was new, well laid out, green and beautifully kept. There had been heavy rains and a storm from the Bay of Biscay and Bayonne smelled fresh and newly washed when the sun came out in the afternoon. The town was packed and there was only one room in the hotel that Antonio and I shared and that we arranged for me to take over when he should leave after the fight. He had to fight at Santander on the west coast of Spain the next day and then go on to Ciudad Real where he and Luis Miguel would fight another mano a mano on August seventeenth. I was going to stay overnight at Bayonne to see Luis Miguel fight on the sixteenth while Antonio fought at Santander and then fly with Miguel to Madrid to go on to Ciudad Real.

The ring had been sold out for several days. The sand was wet and heavy although the sun was bright and the day gray. The bulls were small by first-class standards and some of the horns had been cut down so severely and then repointed and polished to look natural that it was impossible for me to take the corrida as a real test between the two men.

Luis Miguel had a bad stiff knee from his tossing at Málaga. It had stiffened during the night and the long plane ride had made it no better. He had no confidence in his underpinning and he had lost his security and he knew it. He could only fake a proper kill. Two of his bulls were difficult and his mastery of the difficult bull was no longer there. His second bull was exceptionally good and he braced himself against his insecurity and pain and worked well with the cape and then made an excellent faena which he finished off with the tricks the public loved and expected from him. He looked very good doing all this work with the muleta. He was rapidly becoming truly tragic, although few people knew it then, but he tried never to limp nor to make excuses in any of his bulls. Luis Miguel killed his one good bull with a sword that went in almost perpendicularly as he arched his arm. But it was in the right place and they gave him both ears. With his last bull he did nothing except suffer gallantly and try to keep it to himself. I was very sorry for him as I believed that he had reached a peak in Málaga that he could never reach again.

In his three bulls Antonio destroyed him mercilessly. Two of his bulls were better than Miguel's but after Miguel's first sad performance with an inferior bull Antonio poured the heat on as though he were a racing driver passing a crippled rival and made another perfect and brilliant performance with cape, muleta, and the sword. He cut both ears. Since Luis Miguel had reacted to this with his good work on the next bull and cut two ears, Antonio stepped up the pace on his next bull and seared Miguel with a performance no one fighting bulls could equal. He gave four times as much as he had to give to beat Miguel. He cut both ears again and the tail after a single estocada. From the fence I could see that he was dropping the sword that tiny touch to make certain. But he was profiling close, sucking in that deep breath from his open mouth and slamming in over the horns after the sword.

Finally when Miguel had been unfortunate with his last bull Antonio was ruthless. He bettered his last performance, made it even more solid and more dangerous, added a few things that he knew that public would like and then tried to go into the very utmost top of the killing notch. He hit bone, tried again and made it and the bull died as the last bull had the day before. He cut both ears and was off for Santander when I got to the room, leaving a muddy pair of fighting shoes on the bathroom floor.

The next evening we sat over drinks in the long twilight on the terrace of the charming Biarritz airport with Miguel and his old friends I had met the day before at lunch and then flew to Madrid in the chartered plane. The next day Luis Miguel and Antonio were to fight mano a mano again at Ciudad Real one hundred and ninety-six kilometers south of Madrid on the border of La Mancha. They were all rough fights but this was to be a bad one and it would be the third mano a mano in four days. The day after Antonio would be fighting in the far north of Spain at Bilbao in the Basque country and Miguel would fight there the day after. Everybody was tired and we all slept until we felt the plane letting down at Barajas.

Since Pamplona Hotch and Antonio had been switching identities. Antonio was very proud of having two distinct identities. One was the man and the other the torero. When he wanted to rest in his private life he took up changing identities with Hotch who he called Pecas or El Pecas, "The Freckles." He admired Hotch and he liked him very much.

"Pecas," he would say. "You are Antonio."

"Good, Pecas," Hotch would reply. "You better get to work on that scenario for Papa's story."

"Tell him I'm working on it now. It's half completed," Antonio would say to me. "What a day I had writing and playing baseball today."

Always at midnight on the day of the corrida Antonio would say, "Now you're Pecas again. I'm Antonio now. Would you like to be Antonio from now on?"

"Tell him he can be Antonio," Hotch would say. "It's perfectly all right with me. But maybe we'd better synchronize our watches to make sure."

Now at the mano a mano in Ciudad Real that we were going to on this day, it was well past midnight. Antonio was going to have Hotch dress in his room in one of his suits and take him into the ring as the substitute matador or sobresaliente who would have to kill the bulls if both Luis Miguel and Antonio were injured. He wanted Hotch to have to be, or anyway to be, Antonio on the day of the fight and during the fight. It was absolutely illegal and I do not know how grave the penalties would be if anyone spotted Hotch. Of course he would not really be the sobresaliente but Antonio wanted him to think he was. He would go in as an extra banderillero for Antonio and everyone would suppose he was the substitute killer.

"Do you want to do it Pecas?" Antonio asked Hotch.

"Naturally," said Hotch. "Who wouldn't?"

"That's my Pecas. You see why I like to be Pecas? Who wouldn't."

At the old and dark hotel with its narrow stairs and rooms with neither shower nor bath we ate a good country meal in the crowded noisy dining room. Ciudad Real was packed with people from all the surrounding villages. It is at the edge of a big wine country and there was much drinking and enthusiasm. Hotch and Antonio dressed in Antonio's small room and it was the most carefree preparation for a bullfight I have ever seen. Miguelillo was dressing them both.

"What do I do exactly?" Hotch asked.

"Do exactly what I do when we are waiting to come out. Juan will place you and see you are all right. Then come in the same way we do and do what I do. Then get behind the barrera and stay with Papa and do exactly as he says."

"What do I do if I have to kill the bulls?"

"What sort of an attitude is that?"

"I just want to know."

"Papa will tell you exactly what to do in English. How can you have any difficulty? Papa will notice anything that I do wrong or that Miguel does wrong. That's his trade. That's how he makes his money. Then he will tell you what we have done wrong and you listen carefully and then not do it. Then he will tell you how to kill the bull and you do it just the way he says."

"Remember you must not make the matadors look bad

in your first appearance Pecas," I said. "It would be unfriendly. At least wait until you've joined the union."

"Can I join the union now?" Hotch asked. "There's money in my wallet."

"Don't think about money," Antonio said when I translated. "Don't worry about the union or any commercial things. Only think about how great you will be and our pride and confidence in you."

Finally I left them to their devotions and went downstairs to see the others.

When they came downstairs Antonio had his same dark, reserved, concentrated before the bullfight face with the eyes hooded against all outsiders. Hotch's freckled face and second baseman's profile was that of a seasoned novillero facing his first great chance. He nodded at me somberly. No one could tell he was not a bullfighter and Antonio's suit fitted him perfectly.

Then we were inside the ring waiting under the arch of the stands by the white-washed brick wall in front of the red gate. Hotch looked perfect standing with his back against the bricks between Antonio and Luis Miguel.

The fight had caught up with Antonio and he was putting himself into the state of nothing that he always had before the gate opened. All bullfighting had caught up with Luis Miguel for a long time. It had been more tense since Málaga.

I moved around seeing how the picadors were mounted and then knew I must go out the gate and around the ring in the callejón to where I should join Miguelillo who would be putting out the gear and wait for Antonio and Hotch when the paseo was finished. I spoke to the banderilleros and to Luis Miguel and Antonio.

Someone came up to me and asked, "Who is the sobresaliente?"

"El Pecas," I said.

"Oh," he nodded his head.

"Suerte, Pecas," I said to Hotch.

He nodded his head slightly. He was trying to get into the state of nothing too.

I walked around the ring to where Miguelillo and his assistant were laying out the fighting capes and the scabbarded swords and folding and fastening the screws into the wooden sticks of the muletas. I took a drink from the water jug and saw the ring would not be full.

"How's Pecas?" Miguelillo asked me.

"Praying in the chapel for the health of the other fighters," I said.

"Take care of him," Domingo Dominguín said to me. "Any bull can jump."

The paseo had started. We were all watching Pecas. He strode with just the right amount of modesty and quiet confidence. I shifted from him to see if Miguel was limping. He was not. He looked good and confident but his face looked saddened as he saw the places in the ring where there were empty seats. Antonio came in looking like a conqueror. He saw the empty seats and dismissed them.

Hotch came into the callejón and stopped by me.

"What do I do now?" he asked in a low tone.

"Stick by me and look intelligent and ready but not too eager."

"Do I know you?"

"Not too well. I've seen you fight. You're no pal."

Luis Miguel's first bull had come into the ring. He'd taken his medium bull first out of a lot of one small, one medium and one big. He was passing him with the cape and did not seem to favor his bad leg. The crowd was cheering at each pass.

Luis Miguel was working the bull out in front of us

with the muleta. He started well, with good style, got better, started to be very good and then the bull began to fade on him from overpic-ing and loss of blood. They had bled him but they did not tire the neck muscles. Luis Miguel had to go in seven times and only killed finally with the second thrust of the descabello sword.

"What was the matter?" Hotch asked.

"Plenty," I said. "Part the bull's fault and part his."

"Is he going to get that way where he can't kill again?"

"I don't know. The bull didn't help him any but he couldn't keep his left hand down and he couldn't slam in."

"Why is it hard to keep the left hand way down?"

"Danger of death."

"I see," said Hotch.

Antonio's first bull had come out and he was giving him the slow, beautiful cape work. But he had taken his small bull first and the public did not take the bull seriously. The bulls were Gamero Civicos from Salamanca and they were an uneven lot. Two small, one quite big and three medium-sized. When Antonio saw they did not take the bull really seriously when he started his classical work with the muleta and gave them the true passes he switched to the Manolete passes that make any bull look good and gave the whole Manolete routine looking out at the crowd as he passed the bull. He killed with a single estocada a touch low and to the side and they gave him an ear.

Luis Miguel's next bull was big and very powerful. He knocked over the horse on his first charge and the picadors tried their best to take the power and the fight out of him. He was so badly hurt that only one pair of banderillas was placed.

Luis Miguel took the bull half destroyed and tried to make a good faena with him. He made some excellent passes but he couldn't link them up except some turning passes when he seemed to be almost leaning on the bull for support as he guided him around.

Luis Miguel finished well and got the sword in up to the hilt and cut the spinal marrow with the descabello sword on his first attempt. They gave him an ear. He went around the ring with it and then saluted the crowd from the center of the ring. Part of the crowd was not enthusiastic and showed it.

Out on the sand Antonio had started the slow magic with the cape. The bull was charging fast and straight and the cape, held delicately, filled and swelled and moved ahead of him at his exact speed only millimeters ahead of the searching horns. Antonio took great care of the bull with the picadors and in the banderillas. With the muleta he started with four passes standing straight as a statue with his feet together, never moving them from the first charge until the bull had finished passing under the muleta with his horns brushing past Antonio's chest for the fourth time. The music started and he commenced to turn the bull around him in slow quarter circles, then half circles and then wind him in full circles.

"It's impossible to do," Hotch said.

"He can do a circle and a half."

"He isn't leaving much of Luis Miguel."

"Miguel will be all right when his leg is sound," I said and hoped it was true.

"This is doing something to him though," Hotch said. "Watch his face."

"It's an awfully good bull," I said.

"It's something else," Hotch said. "Antonio isn't human. He does things all the time no human being can do. Look at Luis Miguel's face."

I looked and it was quiet, sad and profoundly troubled.

"He's seeing ghosts," Hotch said.

Antonio finished, squared the bull, sighted, took a deep breath and went in over the horns the muleta low and dragging. He killed with a single sword thrust that went in to the pommel and the bull went over dead. They cut both ears and the tail and gave them to him. He came by us and grinned at me and looked at Hotch as though he did not see him. I went over to speak to him.

"Tell Pecas he's looking great." He said the last words in English. "Have you told him how to kill yet?"

"Not yet."

"Tell him."

I went back to Hotch and we watched Luis Miguel's bull come out. It was his small one.

"What did Antonio say?"

"He said you were looking great."

"That's easy," said Hotch. "What else?"

"For me to tell you how to kill."

"It would be useful to know. Do you think I'll have to?"

"I don't think so unless you want to pay to kill the reserve bull."

"What would it cost?"

"Forty thousand pesetas."

"Can I charge it on my Diners Club card?"

"Not in Ciudad Real."

"I'd better pass it up then," Hotch said. "I never carry more than twenty dollars cash. You learn that on the coast."

"I can let you take the money."

"That's all right Papa. I'll only kill if I have to kill for Antonio."

Luis Miguel was working alone with his bull a few paces out from us. They were both doing their best but neither of them, after Antonio's work, was appealing to more than their personal friends and the bull's personal friends were not present. He was showing how a good built to order and to measure Salamanca bull should behave and Miguel was showing how he and Manolete used to thrill them with the made to order stuff before a Miura stretched his neck a little too far and did away with Manolete. The bull got tired of it and slipped from half-bullhood into tiredness and despair. His tongue was out. He had complied with his part of the contract and he needed the sword now as a gift to end it. But Luis Miguel extracted four more Manoletinas from him before he squared him up to kill. He did not go in with much faith and his leg dragged. The sword dropped out. He pulled himself together and went in quite well and the bull went down from tiredness, part of a sword blade, a new thing for him to feel inside him, and from despair. He had done everything he had been bred to do and it had been a disappointment to all.

"Luis Miguel looks in bad shape," Hotch said. "He was so wonderful at Málaga."

"He shouldn't be fighting," I said. "But he wants to fight out of it. He nearly got killed at Valencia. Again at Málaga. That big bull nearly had him today. He's getting sort of preoccupied now."

"What's he preoccupied about?"

"Death," I said. It was all right to say it in English if you said it low. "Antonio carries it around for him in his pocket."

Antonio had taken his biggest bull for the last and he was being as pitiless with Miguel as always. The cape work had the same witchcraft touch and was closer and slower and more unbelievable. The crowd did not understand it but they believed in it and no other cape handling could ever mean the same thing to them again. Antonio kept the bull in good shape for the muleta. Then he showed them all the great passes and how they should be made; making them closer and closer until it seemed no man could make a bull's horns come so close to his body. He circled the bull around him until he was blood-soaked as the bull moved past controlled by his extended arm. He did the passes that Miguel had done and put back all the danger and emotion that had died with Manolete at Linares. He knew they were not as danger-ous as the old passes but he put into them all that they had ever been and more.

Antonio furled the muleta slowly in front of the bull, sighted with the sword pointed for the highest part be-tween the shoulder blades, opened his pursed lips and took a deep breath and went in hard and solid over the horn. The bull was dead when the palm of his hand hit the top of the black shoulders and as he stood free and looked at him, raising his right hand, the bull's legs gave under him, he swayed and went over with a thud.

"Well you didn't have to kill," I said to Hotch.

Miguel was standing looking across the ring at noth-ing. There was the usual hysteria in the crowd and ev-eryone who owned one was waving a handkerchief until both ears had been cut, then the tail and finally a hoof. One ear used to mean the bull was given to the matador by the President to sell for meat and all the rest of the cutting is excessive, as a scale to judge the extent of a triumph. But it was established now along with many other things that do bullfighting no good.

Antonio beckoned for Hotch.

"Go on out and take the tour with the outfit," I said. Hotch loped out and circled the ring with Joni, Ferrer and Juan following behind Antonio with modesty and decorum. It was a little irregular but Antonio had in-vited him. In keeping with his dignity as a sobresaliente he neither threw back hats nor kept cigars. Few who looked at him could doubt that he, "El Pecas," would have been capable of taking over the corrida if it had been necessary. It shone in his rugged honest face and you could see it in the way he moved. In all the plaza only Luis Miguel had noticed that he wore no pigtail. But if he had gone in with a bull the absence of the pigtail would not have been noticed after the bull made his first move. They would have thought it came off the first time he went up in the air.

When Bill and I climbed the stairs up to the little room in the hotel Antonio was soaked in blood. Miguelillo was pulling off his trousers and his long-tailed linen shirt was wet through with blood and clung heavily to his belly and thighs. "Very hard on shirts, Papa," Antonio said to me.

He was going to drive that night to Bilbao after eating in Madrid to sleep there and fight the next afternoon. We would meet at Bilbao at the Carlton.

Antonio wanted to go to Bilbao now, the most difficult public in Spain where the bulls are the biggest and the public the most severe and exigent so that no one could ever say that there was ever anything doubtful or shady or dubious about this campaign of 1959 when he was fighting as no one had fought real bulls since Joselito and Belmonte. If Luis Miguel wanted to go too that was fine. But it would be a dangerous trip. If Luis Miguel had been managed by his father, who was wise and cynical and knew the odds, instead of by his two nice brothers, who needed the ten percent from him and from Antonio each time they fought, he would never have gone to Bilbao to be destroyed.

CHAPTER
13

WE WERE LATE IN GETTING OFF FROM MADRID BUT THE Lancia which we had named "La Barata," the cheap one, made wonderful time and ate up the familiar road to the north. We stopped at the old tavern in Burgos so our ex-driver Mario, who had driven the Lancia down from Udine, Italy, before the mano a mano at Ciudad Real, could eat the trout from the stream in the high Castillian hills beyond the town. Shiny and spotted, they were plump and fresh and firm-fleshed and you could pick out your own trout and partridges in the kitchen. The wine was served in stone pitchers and we had the delicate Burgos cheese I used to bring back to Gertrude Stein in Paris when I'd come home from Spain in the old days third-class on the train.

Mario made it very fast from Burgos to Bilbao. He was a racing driver so it was safe, in theory, but the rev counter could bring the sweat out on my sides when I looked at it. There were three kinds of horns on La

Barata. One meant open up we're coming through. It worked quite well, but after we were past I'd see donkeys and goats and their owners still watching for the train to come.

Bilbao is an industrial and shipping town set down in a cup of hills on a river. It is big, rich, solid, and either hot and moist or cold and moist. There is beautiful country out from it and the small tidewater rivers that cut far back into the country are lovely. It is a big money town and sporting town and I have many friends there. It can be hotter in August than any place in Spain except Córdoba. On this day it was hot but not too hot and clear and the wide streets looked cheerful.

We had good rooms at the Carlton which is an excellent hotel. Bilbao is a very solid, heavy, monied feria like no other in Spain and the bullfighters wear coats and neckties. We had been on the road so long we felt out of place in the smart lobby but La Barata saved our social status. She was the best-looking car in town.

Antonio was in the same happy mood as when we had left him. He liked Bilbao and its stuffiness and heavy richness did not bother him at all. Here no one could go in the callejón. They even ushered the bullfighters out who had fought there the day before and would be fighting the day after. There was more law and authority in evidence than any other place in Spain and police took pleasure in making us walk all the way around the ring rather than enter by the obvious sensible entry that had always been used before.

We got to our places finally and it was odd to see a bullfight from the seats instead of from the barrera. Antonio turned on everything, as he had done all season and was superb with both his bulls. He cut both ears of his two bulls which is all the cutting that is permitted in

Bilbao. Everything looked easy and simple as he did it perfectly and naturally and he killed with the same ease and decision.

Antonio had enchanted the crowd and moved them very deeply. A man sitting next to me said, "He brings back my old feeling about bullfighting that was gone completely." Antonio was happy with his bulls and was able to communicate this happiness to the public who were completely happy with him. It was as though it had all become beautiful and simple to everyone.

Luis Miguel's fight the next day was a great disappointment. He started out well and made two beautiful veronicas on his first bull after a few passes with the cape that were better than fair. In his competition with Antonio his cape work had improved steadily and in the early part of the fight he looked steady and sound. The bull was medium-sized; not bad to work with, but not a gift. Miguel did not look happy, but he did not look bad. He hit bone twice going in well and then got about three-quarters of the sword in and the bull died of it.

His second bull was big with good horns. Luis Miguel kept up his good cape work but the bull was difficult and potentially very dangerous. He hesitated in his charges on the horses and the picadors were hesitant about picing him. Finally it looked as though the bull would come to Luis Miguel head high, difficult and practically unpiced. So the last picador to take him really leaned on him twisting and cutting him up for all he was worth. He could only have done it under orders.

The bull came to Luis Miguel more difficult than when he had first faced the horses and Luis Miguel worked intelligently, but worried now about his leg, to try to dominate him, line him up and get rid of him. The bull was looking for him all the time under the cloth. Luis Miguel went in twice with precautions and little faith. The bull was not to be trusted and Luis Miguel's leg dragged on the take-off. On the third try he got a little over half of the sword blade in but it was in a deadly place and the bull went down. The crowd was disappointed and showed it.

Everyone felt bad about Luis Miguel but Tamames, his doctor, felt the worst. Miguel's wound from Valencia had been bothering him and its pain, dull and sporadic, had put the wound and the circumstances under which he received it back into his mind. The confidence of Málaga was gone and his leg, where he had been tossed in Málaga, was getting worse the more he used it. The injury was to the semi-lunar cartilage. It was the type of injury a football player gets if he is clipped from the side or a baseball player if he hooks a spike into a base and is thrown. Tamames was trying to reduce the inflammation of the cartilage with ultrasonic rays. If it did not reduce but became more inflamed the knee might lock unexpectedly. That could kill Luis Miguel. If the cartilage was removed he might be immobilized for three to six weeks and it was always possible, although not probable, that he might be finished as a bullfighter. So far the cartilage had not gotten bad enough or caused enough damage by its wear and irritation on the two main bones of the leg for locking to be imminent; but it was painful and it destroyed Luis Miguel's confidence.

I was very worried about Luis Miguel. But he insisted on keeping on with the duel with Antonio. After seeing him fight this last time and remembering what had happened in every fight between them from Valencia on I was sure it would only end with Luis Miguel dead or destroyed as a matador. Seeing the way Antonio was fighting and his absolute confidence and mastery I could not admit the possibility of his being gored again. I always sweated him out. But it did not figure that he should be gored now as nearly all gorings show themselves in advance and none was showing either mentally, physically or tactically. He was in a definite stage of flood, of overflow, of "too much." But too much was now his normal state and he was doing it all within the rules that say how it should be done. Fighting perfectly, that is, slowly and beautifully, is always supremely dangerous. But he had such command of all bulls now that everything seemed easy for him and by throwing the fear of death away he had gained something which seemed to armor him.

The feria of Bilbao was very dangerous for Antonio though because he had too many rich and important friends there and there was too much social life. It was not the sinister social life of Madrid. But he stayed up too late and we were not getting the good tiring exercise nor having the exhaustion of the road trips that takes its place and makes a matador get his sleep.

This showed in his fight the day before his last fight with Luis Miguel. Neither of his bulls was good and his last bull went nearly blind in the course of the fight and did not see truly well when he came into the ring. Neither bull was suitable for good cape work nor for a proper faena with the muleta and the first bull was dangerous with a tendency to trot and to keep searching for the man under the cloth. It was no bull to be confident with when working with the cape. But there was more daylight between Antonio and the bull when he passed him with the cape than there would have been if he had been in bed by midnight.

For two days it had been raining in the morning in Bilbao and then it would clear in time for the corrida. The Bilbao ring drains well and they knew the sort of climate they have and the type of sand they would need when they built it. On this day the surface was damp but not slippery even though at noon it had looked as though the fight might be rained out. But the sun came out finally and then there was the heavy damp heat and the passing clouds.

Luis Miguel felt better from the treatments Tamames had been giving him but he was sad and preoccupied. A year ago on this day his father had died after atrocious suffering from cancer and Luis Miguel was thinking about that and about other things. He had the same courtesy as always but he had become much gentler in adversity. He knew how close he had been to being killed when he had fought with Antonio in the last big fights. He knew these Palhas were nothing like the old Palhas that were super Miuras and he knew this town was not Linares. But too many things were piling up and he was running out of luck. It was one thing to live to be the number one in the world in his profession and have that be the one true belief in his life. It was another thing to be almost killed each time he went out to prove it and to know that only his wealthiest and most powerful friends, a number of beautiful women, and Pablo Picasso who had not seen a bullfight in Spain in twenty-five years still believed it. The important thing was for him to believe it himself. The others all could come back if he believed it and could make it true. Hurt and wounded as he was this wasn't a good day to make it true. But he was going to try and maybe the old miracle that he had made at Málaga would come again.

In his room Antonio was calm and relaxed as a leopard resting under the sheet on the bed. We only stayed a very few minutes because I wanted him to rest. But it was happy as it had been all summer.

Down on the main floor the bar and dining room were packed with many people waiting for tables. We finally ate at a big table with many old and new friends. Domingo Domínguín told me he thought the Palhas would be much better than they had been at Valencia. Two were a little light in weight but they looked bigger than they were. They paired up in fairly even lots. Luis Miguel was taking his smaller bull first. The ring was absolutely full and there were many high dignitaries of the government present. Doña Carmen Polo de Franco, the wife of the head of the state, was in the presidential box with a party from San Sebastián.

Luis Miguel's first bull came out fast. He was handsome with good horns and looked bigger than he was. Luis Miguel took him with the cape and made several good passes. His first quite was excellent too. His bad leg did not seem to affect him at all but he seemed sad when he came close to the barrera.

With the muleta he worked close to the bull and made some good right-hand passes. They got better as he went along and he became very confident with the bull. I kept watching his footwork and worrying but everything looked sound. Luis Miguel took the muleta in his left hand and made a series of naturales. They were all right for any other matador but they did not look like the ones of Málaga and only the expensive side of the ring applauded. They asked for music and Luis Miguel made a series of the profile passes that Manolete popularized and did them very well. Then he fixed the bull with a couple of swinging passes that kept his head up and mesmerized him and then knelt down in front of the bull.

Some of the public liked it and some of them did not. Antonio had, temporarily, educated them out of a taste for this sort of thing. Luis Miguel got to his feet without having to use the muleta stick to push up with and the leg was behaving well. He looked tight-lipped and disillusioned. He went in to kill fairly well and straight. The sword was placed quite high but the bull began to bleed from the mouth. He went over in a crash and there was no ear given. The sword looked well placed to me, and there is often mouth bleeding when an artery is severed by a high thrust. There was much applause and Luis Miguel went out and saluted. He was somber and un-smiling. But his leg was working well or he would never have gone down on his knees.

Antonio's bull came out. He was almost identical with Luis Miguel's and about the same size. He was good on both sides and Antonio took him over just where he had stopped the day before. It was the same majestic, beauti-ful cape work we had seen all season, and you could feel the happiness come back in the murmuring of the crowd between the sudden shouts.

After a single pair of banderillas were in he asked permission to take the bull and commenced to build him up with the muleta. The bull was a little slow in charg-ing and Antonio had to move well in onto him. After he had given him confidence with a series of right-hand passes that did not punish him at all but moved him close, closer and then closest, the music started and An-tonio took the bull out and cited him from a distance with the muleta in his left hand. He had lighted him up nicely now and had lengthened the distance at which he would charge.

The bull saw well at a distance and Antonio let him come and then led him with his wrist keeping the cloth moving slowly at just the speed that would hold him through a series of naturales that were close, slow and perfect. He finished with a pass that took the bull's horns past his chest and I watched the red cloth of the muleta clear the horns and then slowly sweep down the neck, shoulders, back and the tail of the bull.

He killed finally, banging in hard and the sword was

in up to the hilt. The sword was well placed, perhaps an inch and a half to the left of the very top of the killing notch and Antonio stood in front of the bull with his right hand raised and watched the bull with his dark gypsy eyes; the hand raised in triumph for the crowd; the body swung back in arrogance for the crowd; but the eyes watching like a surgeon until the bull's hind legs quivered, then commenced to go and he fell over dead.

Then he swung around and looked at the crowd and the surgeon's look was gone from his eyes and his face was happy about the work he had done. A bullfighter can never see the work of art that he is making. He has no chance to correct it as a painter or a writer has. He cannot hear it as a musician can. He can only feel it and hear the crowd's reaction to it. When he feels it and knows that it is great it takes hold of him so that nothing else in the world matters. All the time he is making his work of art he knows that he must keep within the limits of his skill and his knowledge of the animal. Those matadors are called cold who visibly show that they are thinking of this. Antonio was not cold and the public belonged to him now. He looked up at them and let them know, modestly but not humbly, that he knew it and as he circled the ring with the ear in his hand he looked at the different segments of Bilbao, a city that he loved, as they stood up as he passed and was happy that he owned them. I looked at Miguel looking out at nothing from the barrera and I wondered if today would be the day or if it would happen on some other day.

Jaime Ostos was superb in his bull which was a little bigger than the first two and an excellent bull to work with. He was excellent with the cape and both sound and brilliant with the muleta. The crowd were very moved by his work and he was given an ear although he had difficulty with the sword.

After Jaime had made his tour of the ring with the ear, the three matadors went up to the presidential box to pay their respects to Doña Carmen Polo de Franco. Luis Miguel, who is a friend of the Generalissimo's son-in-law and shoots with the head of the state, had sent his compliments and his excuses. But his leg felt well enough for him to go up to the high box. Or if it did not he still went up anyway and then he had to come down again. The next bull was his.

It was a black bull a little bigger than his first. His horns were good and he came in strong and well. Luis Miguel went out with the cape and made four slow, sad veronicas and then wrapped the bull around his waist in a media veronica.

But Luis Miguel did not stay sad. One of his greatest assets had always been his knowledge of how to run a bullfight and direct every move in the fighting of his own bulls. He was going to get everything he could out of this bull and he took him with the cape and fixed him in the exact place from where he wanted him to charge the picador. The picador advanced and raised his pike pole and the bull charged. The picador hit him as he hit the horse, seemed to rectify the position of the pic a little as the bull recharged, and Luis Miguel took the bull out and again made four slow sad veronicas with their solemn ending.

Then he brought the bull back to place him in position to charge again. It is one of the simplest moves in bullfighting and he had done it many thousands of times. He wanted to fix the bull with a flick of his cape with the bull's forefeet outside the painted circle. But as he moved in front of the horse, facing the bull with his back toward the horse and its rider, who held his lance extended, the bull charged the horse and Luis Miguel was in his line of charge. The bull paid no attention to the cape and

sank his horn into Luis Miguel's thigh and threw him
solidly toward the horse. The picador hit the bull with
his lance while Luis Miguel was still in the air. The bull
caught Luis Miguel in the air and as he fell chopped at
him several times on the sand. Domingo, his brother, had
jumped the fence to drag him away. Antonio and Jaime
Ostos had both gone in with their capes to take the bull
away. Everyone knew it was a big and grave wound and
it looked as though it had gone into the abdomen. Most
people thought he had a mortal wound. If he had been
pinned against the back of the horse with its mattress
covering it would almost certainly have been and the
horn would probably have gone through him. His face
was gray as they carried him along the callejón, he was
biting his lips and his hands were across his lower abdomen.

There was no way to get to the infirmary from where
we sat in the first row of seats and the police would not
allow anyone in the passageway so I stayed and watched
while Antonio took over Luis Miguel's bull.

The usual thing, when a bull has given a matador such
a severe and perhaps deadly wound as this one appeared
to be, is for the matador who inherits the bull to work
him briefly and kill him as quickly as possible. Antonio
was having no part of this. It was a good bull and he
would not waste him. The public had paid to see Luis
Miguel. He had been eliminated in a stupid way. This
was his public. If they did not have Dominguín they
could have Ordóñez.

I prefer to think of it this way or that he was living up
to Luis Miguel's contract for him. Anyway, not knowing
how grave the wound was except that it was in the top
of the right thigh and very bad, he went out with his
nerves as quiet and calm as they had been on his last bull
and worked the bull that had just wounded Luis Miguel.

The applause started and the music came and Antonio warmed to the bull and began to make his passes incredibly close. He did an excellent faena and then killed quickly, going in well, but the sword a good two inches off from the high notch. The crowd applauded him. But he knew he had aimed for where he did to kill quickly.

Word came through from the operating room that the wound was in the lower right groin in exactly the same place as the wound received in Valencia. It had gone up into the abdomen but they did not know yet if there was any perforation. Luis Miguel had been anaesthetized and they were operating.

Then Antonio's bull came out. He was the biggest bull so far. He had good horns and he came out as though he were worthless, staring around him and moving at a trot. Juan offered him the cape and he shied away from it and promptly jumped the fence into the passageway and then shouldered and hooked his way along until the open gate let him back into the ring. But when the picadors came out he was brave in charging the horses. The picadors held him off well and he pushed hard under the pics, digging in with his hooves and driving against the steel point. Antonio moved way in on him and got him started on the cape and passed him as though he had no defects. He was measuring his charging speed to the millimeter and adjusting the cape to it and taking command of the bull. But to the public the passes looked the same effortless, magic, slow swings as always.

In banderillas you could see how the bull could learn to be difficult and dangerous and I thought I saw him starting to go to pieces and I sweated out the delay until Antonio should take him with the muleta and the sword. He was sweating it too I could see, although I could not hear from the seat what he was saying to Ferrer and Joni.

While we watched and the public marvelled and

shouted, exploding at each pass and applauding at the
end of each series, Antonio, with the music playing, led
the bull, who had seemed only big, nervous, churlish and
worthless, through a complete course of everything classic and beautiful that a man could do with a brave bull.
There was no daylight now ever between him and the
animal as the horns passed his body. He would bring the
bull in at the bull's chosen speed and the control of his
wrist over the hanging red serge cloth would form the
plastic figure when the great bulk and the erect, lithe
figure joined and completed their turn. Then the wrist
would turn and bring the heavy black bull with the
death in his horns past his chest again in the last and
most dangerous and difficult figure of all. Seeing him do
this pase de pecho again and again I was sure of what he
was going to do. It all felt like great music but it was not
an end in itself. He was preparing the bull to kill him
recibiendo.

The greatest way to kill, if the bull can still charge, is
recibiendo. It is the oldest and the most dangerous and
the most beautiful since the matador instead of running
in on the bull stands quietly, provokes the bull's charge
and then, when the bull comes, guides him past and to
the right with the muleta while he puts the sword in
high between the bull's shoulders. It is dangerous because if the muleta does not control the bull perfectly
and he raises his head the matador receives the horn
wound in his chest. The usual horn wound, if the bull
raises his head as the man goes in to kill, is in the right
thigh. In killing recibiendo, to kill properly the man
must wait the charge out until the bull will get him if he
waits an inch to two inches more. If he leans outside, or
if he gives the bull too wide an exit as he swings the
cloth, the sword will go in sideways.

"Wait until he is going to get you," is the axiom for
killing in this way. Few people can wait it out and also

have the great left hand to guide the bull out low and clear. It is basically the same pass, for the bull, that the pase de pecho is and that was why Antonio was preparing the bull with these passes and making sure that he still had the drive to follow the cloth and would not raise his head up or stop and hesitate in the middle of the encounter. When he saw the bull was ready and intact he squared him up below us and prepared to kill.

We had talked in the long rides at night about this way of killing and had agreed that for Antonio with his left hand it was easy. It was only the penalty that made it difficult. The penalty was the driving of the horn like a dagger thrust up into the chest with the dagger as big around as a broom stick driven by neck muscles that could lift and throw a horse or splinter the two-inch planks of the barrera. Sometimes these horns had points that could slit the silk facing of a cape like a razor. Sometimes they would be splintered so that any wound they would make could be as wide as your hand. It was easy all right if you could wait quietly to see them come directly toward you and know you had to wait until they would surely get you in the chest coming up from below if the bull raised his head when he felt the steel going into him. Sure it was easy. We agreed on that.

So now Antonio drew himself up, sighted along the blade of the sword, and bent his left knee forward as he swung the muleta toward the bull. The big bull charged, the sword hit bone high up between the shoulders. Antonio leaned in onto the bull, the sword buckled, the group that should have been united broke apart and the sweep of the muleta swung the bull clear.

No one in our time cites twice recibiendo. That belongs to the times of Pedro Romero, that other great torero of Ronda who lived years ago. But Antonio had to kill him in this way as long as he would charge. So he squared him up again, sighted along the blade, and invited him in again with leg and cloth and brought him in to where he would have to get him if the head came up. Again the sword hit bone, again the group confused and broke up and again the muleta guided the horns and the big bull clear.

The bull was slowed now but Antonio knew he had one more clean charge in him. He had to know it but no one else did and the crowd could not believe what they were seeing. All Antonio had to do to have a great triumph with this bull was to have put a sword into him decently without too much exposure. But he was going to make up for every bull he had taken any advantage of in killing through all his life; and there were plenty of them. This bull had been given two free shots at his chest if he had wanted to take them and now he would give him a third one. He could have slipped the sword in a little bit low or to one side each time the bull had come and no one would have held it against him when he killed recibiendo. He knew where it was soft and went in fast and still looked good, or good enough, or anyway not bad. That was the kind of kill most ears were given on in these years of bullfighting. But the hell with that today. Today he was going to pay out for every advantage he had ever taken of any bull with the sword.

He squared the bull up and the plaza was so quiet I could hear the click behind me as a woman's fan closed. Antonio sighted along the blade of the sword, bent his left knee forward, swung the muleta toward the bull and as the bull came he waited until the exact moment when the horns would get him, and then the point of the sword went in and the bull came pushing on it, his head down following the red cloth and Antonio's flat palm was pushing on the pommel and the blade slid in slowly high up between the very top of the shoulder blades. Antonio's feet had not moved and the bull and he were one now and when his hand came flat onto the top of the black hide the horn had passed his chest and the bull was dead under his hand. The bull did not know it yet and he watched Antonio standing before him with his hand raised, not in triumph but as though to say good-bye. I knew what he was thinking but for a minute it was hard for me to see his face. The bull could not see his face either but it was a strange friendly face of the strangest boy I ever knew and for once it showed compassion in the ring where there is no place for it. Now the bull knew that he was dead and his legs failed him and his eyes were glazing as Antonio watched him fall.

That was how the duel between Antonio and Luis Miguel ended that year. There was not any true rivalry anymore to anyone who was present in Bilbao. The question was settled. It could be revived, but only technically. It could be revived on paper or to make money or to exploit the South American public. But there was not any question anymore who was the best if you had seen the fights and if you had seen Antonio at Bilbao. Sure maybe he was only the best at Bilbao because Luis Miguel had a bad leg. Maybe there could always be some money made out of that assumption. But it would be much too dangerous and deadly to ever try to test it out again before a real public in a Spanish ring with real bulls with real horns. It was something that had been settled and I was happy when the word came from the operating room that once again while the horn had gone well up into the abdomen of Luis Miguel it had not perforated the intestines.

That night when he was dressed Antonio and I drove out to see Luis Miguel. Antonio was driving. He was not cooled out from the fight and we talked about it up in the room and then in the car.

"How did you know he had enough gas to come the second and the third times?" I asked.

"I knew it," he said. "How do you know anything?"

"But what could you see?"

"I knew him very well by then."

"His ear?"

"Everything. I know you. You know me. Like that. Didn't you think he'd come?"

"Sure. But I was in the stands. It's a long way away."

"It's only six or eight feet but it's really a mile," he said.

In Luis Miguel's room at the clinic he was in much pain. The horn had gone into the scar tissue of the old wound from Valencia that was not completely healed and ripped it open, then followed the trajectory of the old wound up into the abdomen. There were half a dozen people in the room and Luis Miguel was being gracious to them through his suffering. His wife was due in with his older sister on a plane from Madrid after midnight.

"I'm sorry I couldn't get to the infirmary," I said. "How's the pain holding?"

"It's so-so, Ernesto," he said very softly.

"Manolo will ease it."

He smiled gently. "He has," he said.

"Can I take any of these people out?"

"Poor people," he said. "You took so many before. I missed you."

"I'll see you in Madrid," I said. "Maybe if we go some of them will go."

"We all look so nice together in the rotogravures," he said.

"I'll see you at Ruber's." Ruber's was the hospital.

"I've kept the apartment," he said.

GLOSSARY

OF
BULLFIGHT TERMS

The definitions that follow are reprinted from Death in the Afternoon by Ernest Hemingway. Used by permission.

AFICIONADO: one who understands bullfights in general and in detail and still cares for them.

ALTERNATIVA: is the formal envesture of an apprentice matador or matador de novillos as a full matador de toros. It consists in the senior matador of the fight giving up his right to kill the first bull and signifying it by presenting muleta and sword to the bullfighter who is alternating for the first time in the killing of bulls with full matadors de toros.

APARTADO: the sorting of the bulls usually at noon before the fight, separating them and putting them in the pens in the order in which it has been decided they are to be fought.

ARENA: the sand which covers the ring.

BANDERILLA: a rounded dowel, seventy centimetres long, wrapped in colored paper, with a harpoon shaped steel point, placed in pairs in the withers of the bull in the second act of the bullfight; the prong of the harpoon catching under the skin. They should be placed high on the very top of the withers and close together.

BANDERILLERO: bullfighter under the orders of the matador and paid by him, who helps run the bull with the cape and places banderillas. Each matador employs four banderilleros who are sometimes called *peónes*. They were once called *chulos*, but that term is no longer used. They take turns placing the banderillas, two of them placing them on one bull and the other two on the next. When travelling, their expenses, except wine, coffee and tobacco, are paid by the matador, who, in turn, collects them from the promoter.

BARRERA: the red painted wooden fence around the sanded ring in which the bull is fought. The first row of seats are also called barreras.

BRÍO: brilliance and vivacity.

BURLADERO: a shelter of planks set close together and a little out from the corral or barrera behind which the bullfighters and herders can dodge if pursued.

CALLEJÓN: the passageway between the wooden fence or barrera which surrounds the ring and the first row of seats.

CAPA or CAPOTE: the cape used in bullfighting. Shaped like the capes commonly worn in Spain in the winter, it is usually made of raw silk on one side and percale on the other, heavy, stiff and reinforced in the collar, cerise colored on the outside and yellow on the inner side. They are heavy to hold and at the lower extremities small corks have been stitched into the cloth of the capes the matadors use. These the matador holds in his hands when he lifts the lower ends of the cape and gathers them together for hand-holds when swinging the cape with both hands.

CAPEA: informal bullfights or bull baitings in village squares in which amateurs and aspirant bullfighters take part. Also a parody of the formal bullfight given in parts of France or where the killing of the bull is prohibited in which no picadors are used and the killing of the bull is simulated.

CHICUELINAS: a pass with the cape invented by Manuel Jiminez "Chicuelo." The man offers the cape to the bull and when the bull has charged and is past, the man, while the bull turns, makes a pirouette in which the cape wraps itself around him. At the conclusion of the pirouette he is facing the bull ready to make another pass.

CHULO: see *banderillero*.

CITAR: challenging the bull's attention to provoke a charge.

CORNADA: a horn wound; a real wound as distinct from a *varetazo* or bruising scratch.

CORRIDA or CORRIDA DE TOROS: the Spanish bullfight.

CUADRILLA: the troupe of bullfighters under the orders of a matador including picadors and banderilleros one of whom acts as puntillero.

DESCABELLAR: to descabello or kill the bull from in front after he has been mortally wounded through an estocade by driving the point of the sword between the base of the skull and the first vertebra so that the spinal cord is severed. This is a *coup de grâce* administered by the matador while the bull is still on his feet. If the bull is nearly dead and carries his head low, the stroke is not difficult since with the head nearly to the ground the space between the vertebra and the skull will be open. However, many matadors not caring to risk going in and passing the horn again if they have administered one estocade, whether mortal or not, try to descabello while the bull is in no sense nearly dead and, since the animal must then be tricked into lowering his head and may chop up with it as he sees or feels the sword, the descabello then becomes difficult and dangerous. It is dangerous both for spectators and matador since the bull with an upward chop of his head will often send the sword thirty or more feet into the air. Swords tossed in this way by bulls have frequently killed spectators in Spanish rings.

In the proper way of descabelloing the muleta is held low on the ground to force the bull to lower his muzzle. The matador may prick the bull's muzzle either with the point of the muleta or with the sword to force him to lower it. When the point of the sword used in this thrust, the blade of which is straight and stiff rather than curved down in the usual way, is properly placed, it strikes and severs the spinal marrow and the bull falls as suddenly as light goes off when a button is turned to extinguish an electric light.

ENCIERRO: the driving of fighting bulls on foot, surrounded by steers, from one corral to the corral of the ring. In Pamplona the running of the bulls through the streets with the crowd running ahead of them from the corral at the edge of the town into and through the bull ring into the corral of the ring. The bulls to be fought in the afternoon are run through the streets at seven o'clock in the morning of the day they are to be fought.

ESPONTÁNEO: see Introduction, p. 25.

ESTOCADA: sword thrust or estocade in which the matador goes in from the front to attempt to place the sword high up between the bull's shoulder blades.

Estoque: the sword used in bullfighting. It has a lead-weighted, chamois-covered pommel, a straight cross guard five centimetres from the pommel and the hilt and cross guard are wrapped in red flannel. The blade is about seventy-five centimetres long and is curved downward at the tip in order that it may penetrate better and take a deeper direction between the ribs, vertebræ, shoulder blades and other bony structure which it may encounter. Modern swords are made with one, two or three grooves or canals along the back of the blade, the purpose of these being to allow air to be introduced into the wound caused by the sword, otherwise the blade of the sword serves as a plug to the wound it makes. The best swords are made in Valencia and their prices vary according to the number of canals and the quality of steel used. The usual equipment for a matador is four ordinary killing swords and one straight-tipped sword with slightly widened point for the descabello. The blades of all these swords except that used for the descabello are ground razor-sharp half way up their length from the tip. They are kept in soft leather sheaths and the complete outfit is carried in a large, usually embossed, leather sword case.

Estribo: metal stirrup of the picador; also the ridge of wood about eighteen inches above the ground which runs around the inside of the barrera which aids the bullfighters in vaulting the wooden fence.

Faena: the sum of the work done by the matador with the muleta in the final third of the bullfight; it also means any work carried out; a *faena de campo* being any of the operations of bull raising.

Fiesta: holiday time or time of enjoyment; *Fiesta de los toros:* the bullfight.

Hombre: man, as an ejaculation expresses surprise,

pleasure, shock, disapproval or delight, according to tone used. *Muy Hombre:* very much of a man.

LARGAS: a pass to draw the bull toward and then send him away from the man made with the cape fully extended and held at extremity by one hand.

LIDIA: the fight; *toro de lidia:* fighting bull. Also the name of the most famous and oldest bullfight weekly.

MANO A MANO: see Introduction, p. 19.

MATADOR: a formal killer of bulls.

MEDIA-ESTOCADA: an estocade in which only half of the blade goes into the bull. If properly placed on a medium-sized bull a media-estocada will kill as quickly as one that goes in the full length. If the bull is very large, however, half a blade may not be long enough to reach the aorta or other large blood vessels, the cutting of which produces death quickly.

MEDIA VERONICA: a recorte, or cutting short of the bull's charge, which ends a series of passes with the cape known as veronicas (see explanation). The media veronica is accomplished by the man holding the cape in both hands, as for the veronica, and as the bull passes the man, moving from left to right, the man brings his left hand close to his hip and gathers the cape toward his hip with his right hand, shortening the swing of the veronica and making the cape swing half full, turning the bull on himself and fixing him in place so that the man may walk away with his back toward the animal. This fixing in place is accomplished by the swirl of the cape cutting the bull's normal course through making him attempt to turn in a shorter distance than his own length. Juan Belmonte was the perfecter of this lance with the cape and it is now the obligatory ending for any series of veronicas. The half passes made by the matador when holding the cape in both hands and running

backward swaying the cape from side to side to take
the bull from one part of the ring to another were
once called *media-veronicas*, but the real media
veronica at present is the one described above.

MOZO DE ESTOQUES: personal servant and sword handler
for the matador. In the ring he prepares the muletas
and hands his master the swords as he needs them,
wiping off the used swords with a sponge and drying
them before putting them away. While the matador
is killing he must follow him around in the passageway to be always opposite him ready to hand him a
new sword or muleta over the barrera as he needs
it. When it is windy he dampens capes and muleta
from a water jug he carries and also looks after all
personal wants of the matador. Outside the ring before the fight he takes around the envelopes containing the matador's card and a certain sum of
money to the different bullfight critics, aids the matador to dress, and sees that all the equipment is tran-
sported to the ring. After the fight he sends the
telefonemas—messages sent by the telephone company and written and delivered as telegrams are in
the United States—or the more rare verbal messages
to the matador's family, friends, the press and any
clubs of bullfight enthusiasts that may be organized
in the matador's name.

MULETA: heart-shaped scarlet cloth of serge or flannel
folded and doubled over a tapered wooden stick
equipped with a sharp steel point at the narrow end
and a grooved handle at the widened extremity; the
sharp point is pricked through the cloth where it is
folded to a point and the loose end is fastened to the
handle with a thumbscrew so that the wood supports
the folds of the cloth. The muleta is used to defend
the man; to tire the bull and regulate the position of

his head and feet; to perform a series of passes of more or less æsthetic value with the bull; and to aid the man in the killing.

NATURAL: pass made with the muleta held low in the left hand, the man citing the bull from in front; with his right leg toward the bull, the muleta held by the centre of the stick in the left hand, left arm extended and the cloth in front of the man, it is swung slightly toward the bull to start him, this swing being almost imperceptible to the spectator; as the bull charges and arrives at the muleta the man turns with him, his arm fully extended and moving the muleta slowly ahead of the bull making him turn in a quarter of a circle around the man; giving a swinging flip imparted with a lift of the wrist at the conclusion of the pass to hold the bull in position for another pass. It is the fundamental pass of bullfighting, the simplest, capable of greatest purity of line and the most dangerous to make.

NOVILLADA: at the present time a novillada is a bullfight in which bulls which are underaged, or overaged, for a formal bullfight, that is, under four years and over five, or defective in vision or horn, are fought by bullfighters who have either never taken or renounced the title of matador de toros. In every way except the quality of the bulls and the inexperience or admitted failure of the bullfighters a novillada or corrida de *novillos-toros* is the same as a regular bullfight. It is in the novilladas that the majority of the bullfighters who die in the ring are killed each year, since men with little experience fight exceedingly dangerous bulls in small towns where the ring often has only rudimentary operating equipment and no surgeon skilled in the very special technique of horn wounds.

NOVILLERO: a matador of novillos-toros, the bulls described above. He may either be an aspirant or a matador who has failed to make a living and renounced his alternative in search of contracts.

NOVILLO: bull used in novilladas.

PASE: pass made with either cape or muleta; movement of the lure to draw a charge by the animal in which his horns pass the man's body.

PASEO: entry of the bullfighters into the ring and their passage across it.

PECHO: chest; the pase de pecho is a pass made with the muleta in the left hand at the finish of a natural in which the bull, having turned at the end of the natural, recharges and the man brings him by his chest and sends him out with a forward sweep of the muleta. The pase de pecho should be the ending of any series of naturales. It is also of great merit when it is used by the bullfighter to liberate himself from an unexpected charge or sudden return of the bull. In this case it is called a *forzado de pecho* or a forced pass. It is called *preparado*, or prepared, when it is given as a separate pass without having been preceded by a natural. The same pass may be done with the right hand, but it is not then a true pase de pecho since the real *natural* and real *de pecho* are done only with the left hand. When either of these passes is done with the right hand the sword, which must always be held in the right hand, spreads the cloth and makes a much bigger lure thus enabling the matador to keep the bull a greater distance away from him and send him further away after each charge. Work done with the muleta held in the right hand and spread by the sword is often very brilliant and meritorious but it lacks the difficulty, danger and sincerity of work done with the muleta in the left hand and the sword in the right.

PEÓN: banderillero; torero who works on foot under the orders of the matador.

PICA: the pic or pike pole used in bullfighting. It is composed of a wooden shaft 2 meters and between 55 and 70 centimeters long made of ash, has a triangular steel point 29 millimeters long. Below the steel point the head of the shaft is wrapped with cord and it is equipped with a round metal guard to prevent its entering more than 108 millimetres into the bull at the very most. The present model of pic is very hard on the bull and bulls which really charge and insist under punishment can rarely accept more than four pics without losing most of their force.

PICADOR: man who pics bulls from on horseback under the orders of the matador. Has his right leg and foot armored under chamois-skin breeches, wears short jacket and a shirt and tie like any other bullfighter, and a wide low-crowned hat with a pompom on the side. Picadors are seldom gored by the bull since the matadors must protect them with their capes when they fall toward the bull. If they fall away from the bull they are protected by the horse. Picadors suffer broken arms, jaws, legs, and ribs frequently, and fractured skulls occasionally. Few are killed in the ring in proportion to matadors, but many suffer permanently from concussion of the brain. Of all ill-paid professions in civil life I believe it is the roughest and the most constantly exposed to danger of death, which, fortunately, is nearly always removed by the matador's cape.

PODER Á PODER: force to force; method of placing banderillas.

PRESIDENCIA: authority in charge of the conduct of the bullfight.

PUNTILLA: dagger used to kill bull or horse after he has been mortally wounded.

PUNTILLERO: man who kills bull with the puntilla.

QUITE: from *quitar*—to take away—is the taking away of the bull from any one who has been placed in immediate danger by him. It especially refers to the taking away of the bull from the horse and man after he has charged the picadors, by the matadors armed with capes and taking their turns in rotation; each one taking the bull after a charge. The matador who is to kill the bull makes the first *quite* and the others follow in order. From going in close with the cape, bringing the bull out and away from fallen horse and man and placing him in position before the next picador the *quite* has changed now so that a series of lances with the cape after taking the bull out is obligatory on a matador each time he makes a *quite;* they supposedly rivalling to see how close and artistically they can pass the bull. *Quites* made to take the bull away from a man he is goring or who is on the ground with the bull over him are participated in by all the bullfighters and it is at this time that you can judge their valor, knowledge of bulls and degree of abnegation since a *quite* in these circumstances is highly dangerous and very difficult to make as the men must get so close to the bull in order to make him leave the object he is trying to gore that their retreat, taking him out with the cape when he charges, is very compromised.

RECIBIR: to kill the bull from in front awaiting his charge with the sword without moving the feet once the charge has started; with the muleta low in the left hand and the sword in the right hand, right forearm across the chest pointing toward the bull and as he comes in and takes the muleta putting the sword in with the right hand and swinging him out with the muleta in the left as in a pase de pecho, not moving the feet until the sword has gone in. Most difficult,

dangerous and emotional way to kill bulls; rarely
seen in modern times.

REDONDEL: synonym for the ring where the bull is
fought.

REDONDO: *En redondo*—are several passes in succession
such as naturals in which the man and the bull
finally execute a complete circle; any pass which
tends to make a circle.

SOBRESALIENTE: when two matadors fight six bulls between them a novillero or aspirant matador makes
the entry with them as sobresaliente or substitute
and is charged with killing the bulls in case both
matadors should be wounded and unable to continue. A sobresaliente is expected to aid with his cape
in the routine work of the placing of the banderillas.
He is usually allowed by the matadors to make one
or two quites toward the end of the fight.

SORTEO: making up the lots and drawing of the bulls
before the fight to determine which bulls shall be
killed by which matadors.

TOREO: the art of fighting bulls. *Toreo de salon:* practic-
ing cape and muleta work for form and style without any bull being present; necessary part of a matador's training.

TORERO: professional bullfighter. Matadors, banderi-
lleras, picadors are all toreros. *Torera* means having
to do with bullfighting.

TORIL: enclosure from which bulls come into the ring
to be fought.

TRUCOS: tricks.

VARA: shaft; pic used in bullfighting.

VERONICA: pass with the cape so called because the cape
was originally grasped in the two hands in the manner in which Saint Veronica is shown in religious
paintings to have held the napkin with which she

wiped the face of Christ. It has nothing to do with the man wiping the face of the bull as one writer on Spain has suggested. In making the veronica the matador stands either facing or profiled toward the bull with left leg slightly advanced and offers the cape which he holds with both hands having grasped the lower front corners of the cape where the corks are attached and raised them, bunching up the material so that he has a good handhold with each hand, the fingers pointing down, the thumb up. As the bull charges the man awaits him until his horns lower to hook the cape at which instant the man moves the cape ahead of the bull's charge with a suave movement of the arms, his arms held low, passing the bull's head and his body past the man's waist. He passes the bull out with the cape pivoting slightly on his toes or the balls of his feet as he does so and at the end of the pass, as the bull turns, the man is in position to repeat the pass his right leg slightly advanced this time, drawing cape ahead of the bull so that he passes by in the other direction. The veronica is tricked by the man making a sidestep as the bull charges to take him further away from the horns, by the man putting his feet together once the horn has passed and by the man leaning or stepping toward the bull once the horn has passed to make it look as though he had passed the horn close. A matador who is not faking the veronica will sometimes pass the bull so close that the horns will pick off the gold rosettes that ornament his jacket. Matadors, too, will sometimes cite the bull with both feet together and make a series of veronicas in this way with the feet as still as though the man were nailed to the ground. This can only be done with a bull that turns and recharges of his own accord and in a perfectly straight line. The feet must be slightly apart in making a bull pass and repass if the bull needs to be made to follow the swing of the cape at the end of the pass in order to turn. In any case the merit in the veronica is not determined by whether the feet are together or apart, but by whether they remain immobile from the moment of the charge until the bull has been passed and the closeness with which the man passes the horn by his body. The slower, suaver and lower the man swings the cape with his arms the better the veronica.

INDEX